CHURCHES OF WARWICKSHIRE

AIDAN McRAE THOMSON

AMBERLEY

Dedicated to my good friend, artist and legend Brett Jones, 1969–2024

This edition first published 2025

Amberley Publishing
The Hill, Stroud
Gloucestershire GL5 4EP

www.amberley-books.com

British Library Cataloguing in Publication Data.
A catalogue record for this book is available from the British Library.

ISBN 978 1 3981 2276 5 (print)
ISBN 978 1 3981 2277 2 (ebook)

Typesetting by SJmagic DESIGN SERVICES, India.
Printed in Great Britain.

Appointed GPSR EU Representative:
Easy Access System Europe Oü, 16879218
Address: Mustamäe tee 50, 10621, Tallinn, Estonia
Contact Details: gpsr.requests@easproject.com, +358 40 500 3575

Contents

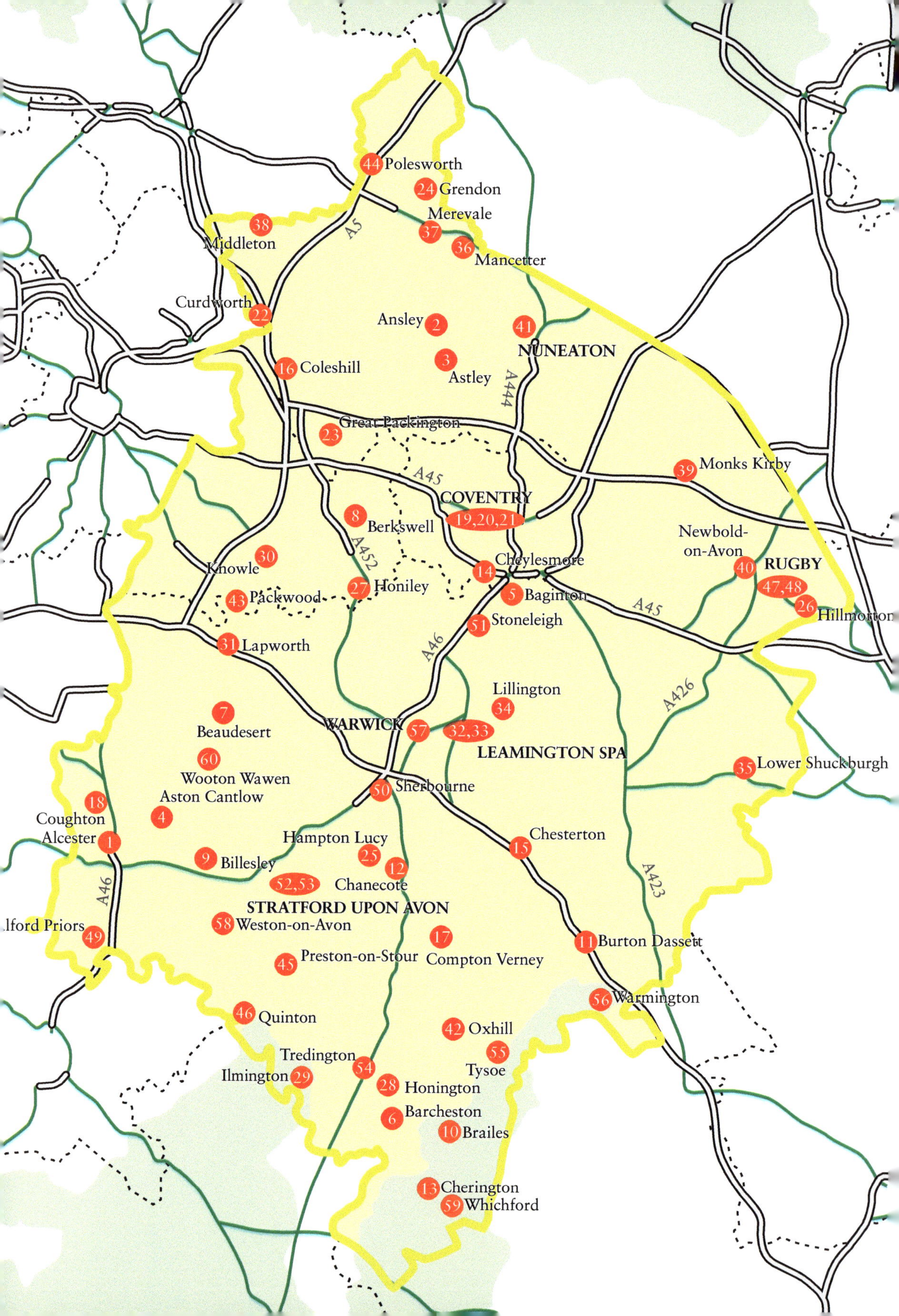

44 Polesworth
24 Grendon
Merevale
37
38
Middleton
36
Mancetter
A5
Curdworth
22
Ansley 2
41
NUNEATON
16 Coleshill
3
Astley
A444
Great Packington
23
39 Monks Kirby
A45
COVENTRY
19,20,21
8
Berkswell
Newbold-
on-Avon
A452
30
Knowle
Cheylesmore
14
40
RUGBY
47,48
27 Honiley
43 Packwood
5 Baginton
26 Hillmorton
A45
51 Stoneleigh
31 Lapworth
A46
Lillington
34
7
Beaudesert
WARWICK
57
32,33
A426
LEAMINGTON SPA
60
Wooton Wawen
35 Lower Shuckburgh
50 Sherbourne
Aston Cantlow
18
Coughton
4
Alcester
1
Hampton Lucy
Chesterton
15
9 Billesley
25
12
A423
52,53
Chanecote
A46
STRATFORD UPON AVON
58 Weston-on-Avon
lford Priors
49
17
11 Burton Dassett
45 Preston-on-Stour
Compton Verney
56 Warmington
46 Quinton
42 Oxhill
55
Tredington
Tysoe
54
Ilmington 29
28 Honington
6 Barcheston
10 Brailes
13 Cherington
59 Whichford

Key

1 Alcester, St Nicholas
2 Ansley, St Laurence
3 Astley, St Mary
4 Aston Cantlow, St John the Baptist
5 Baginton, St John the Baptist
6 Barcheston, St Martin
7 Beaudesert, St Nicholas
8 Berkswell, St John the Baptist
9 Billesley, All Saints
10 Brailes, St George
11 Burton Dassett, All Saints
12 Charlecote, St Leonard
13 Cherington, St John the Baptist
14 Cheylesmore, Christ Church
15 Chesterton, St Giles
16 Coleshill, SS Peter and Paul
17 Compton Verney, Chapel
18 Coughton, SS Peter and Paul
19 Coventry, Cathedral
20 Coventry, Holy Trinity
21 Coventry, St John the Baptist
22 Curdworth, St Nicholas
23 Great Packington, St James
24 Grendon, All Saints
25 Hampton Lucy, St Peter ad Vincula
26 Hillmorton, St John the Baptist
27 Honiley, St John the Baptist
28 Honington, All Saints
29 Ilmington, St Mary
30 Knowle, St John the Baptist, St Lawrence and St Anne
31 Lapworth, St Mary
32 Leamington Spa, All Saints
33 Leamington Spa, St Mark
34 Lillington, Our Lady
35 Lower Shuckburgh, St John the Baptist
36 Mancetter, St Peter
37 Merevale, Our Lady
38 Middleton, St John the Baptist
39 Monks Kirby, St Edith
40 Newbold-on-Avon, St Botolph
41 Nuneaton, St Nicholas
42 Oxhill, St Lawrence
43 Packwood, St Giles
44 Polesworth, St Edith
45 Preston on Stour, St Mary
46 Quinton, St Swithin
47 Rugby, St Andrew
48 Rugby, School Chapel
49 Salford Priors, St Matthew
50 Sherbourne, All Saints
51 Stoneleigh, St Mary
52 Stratford-upon-Avon, Holy Trinity
53 Stratford-upon-Avon, Guild Chapel of the Holy Cross
54 Tredington, St Gregory
55 Tysoe, Assumption
56 Warmington, St Michael
57 Warwick, St Mary
58 Weston-on-Avon, All Saints
59 Whichford, St Michael
60 Wootton Wawen, St Peter

Introduction

The purpose of this book is to introduce some of the finest and most representative churches of Warwickshire, the geographical centre of England. Being a fairly small county (with some 245 active Anglican churches listed in the diocese of Coventry), making a selection of the best churches has been an easier task than it might have been. Additionally, the county's administrative borders were changed in 1974, leaving the historical county reduced in size by the loss of Birmingham, Coventry and the intervening areas to form the bulk of the newly created county of West Midlands. The detachment of Coventry and the adjoining area to the west, however, effectively ripped out the historical heart of the county, thus for the purpose of this book it makes sense to retain them, though Birmingham and its suburbs will be omitted here to feature in a separate volume.

Warwickshire is a difficult county to define architecturally, and its parish churches range from the simplest of rural sanctuaries to some of the most impressive in the entire country. This broad spectrum is also reflected in the building materials, the colour of which gives so much character to each individual church. Given its predominance in the West Midlands, one could be forgiven for thinking of Warwickshire as a red-sandstone county, and yet the use of various red sandstones is mostly confined to the west and north; there is also much use of grey sandstones in these areas. The south and eastern areas, however, feature everything from a friable white lias to rich, caramel-coloured ironstones in the south-east and even Cotswold limestone in the south-west. The result is an attractive and unusually varied palette across the county. However, these varied hues have come at a cost since Warwickshire's local stones (the red and grey sandstones in particular) have not resisted time and weather well, which has necessitated much restoration and renewal.

Christianity was established in the area in AD 653 when it was still the heart of the kingdom of Mercia, having been brought by missionaries from Northumbria. The earliest extant evidence of church building in Warwickshire dates from rather later in the Anglo-Saxon period, though very little in the county has survived from before the Norman Conquest (the most significant remnant being the base of the tower at Wootton Wawen). By the Norman period there were around thirty parishes in the county, and examples of Romanesque architecture are represented at a few locations, most notably the chancel and crypt at Berkswell (along with superb carved fonts at Coleshill, Curdworth and Stoneleigh), though most of the churches of Norman origin have since been modified beyond recognition. The vast majority of Warwickshire's parish churches date from the medieval period, at which point the tally of parishes rose to well over 200 (most of which remain in use to this day) and cover all the evolutionary styles of English Gothic up to the Tudor period: Early English, Decorated and Perpendicular, with the latter perhaps the best represented, most notably in the major civic churches of Coventry, Stratford and Warwick.

Naturally, the Reformation had as huge an impact on the county's religious heritage as it did elsewhere with the closure of all monastic houses, thus the thirty or so establishments across Warwickshire, each with their own grand churches, were swiftly swept away, the biggest casualty being the loss of Coventry's Cathedral of St Mary (the only medieval English cathedral destroyed at this time). A few of the smaller abbey and priory churches were retained in part at least to serve parish use, thus the present churches of Atherstone, Monks Kirby, Polesworth and Wroxall embody the last vestiges of a lost monastery (to which can be added Merevale church, a rare example of a 'chapel before the gate' of the lost abbey). Collegiate foundations (non-monastic but served by a college of canons) were also suppressed, but their churches at Stratford and Warwick already served parish use and thus remained, while Astley was for a short time abandoned due to its remoteness, but its chancel was revived as a glorious fragment.

The most serious impact of the Protestant Reformation on each individual church was a visual one as state-sanctioned iconoclasm (particularly under the reign of Edward VI) resulted in the loss of vast quantities of medieval art and furnishings, leaving interiors denuded of their ornaments and painted walls whitewashed, stark and bare. Stained glass often fared better given its structural role, but alas most succumbed to vandalism during the Civil War in the 1640s, and much of what remained was then lost to neglect in the following century. Fortunately, we are blessed with the survival of perhaps the best pre-Reformation church interior in the country in the Beauchamp Chapel at St Mary's, Warwick, where a remarkable display of sculpture and much fine glass survive to give a tantalising hint of what we have lost elsewhere.

Normally a selection of a county's finest churches would consist almost exclusively of buildings from the Middle Ages (and a few earlier ones perhaps) but some especially fine examples of late seventeenth century and Georgian baroque are also to be found, with especially fine examples at Honiley and Honington. By the time of the Gothic Revival in the early nineteenth century there had been a significant increase in population and industrialisation that saw new parishes formed in urban areas, with Leamington Spa and Rugby especially well endowed with ambitious Victorian churches on an unusually grand scale.

The increase of population and industry also generated a higher degree of wealth in the Victorian period, and this is reflected in the level of attention churches in Warwickshire received from restorers at the time. With churches already more vulnerable to the effects of time owing to the use of softer local sandstones a degree of renewal was inevitable, but the hand of the Victorian restorer has in general fallen more heavily on Warwickshire than most counties, even in the more remote villages. It is easy to criticise the overzealous nature of interventions at this time, and we should remember that such work done was usually done with good intentions and in many cases saved neglected or dilapidated buildings from ruination. The result, however, is that most church interiors are now largely dominated by Victorian 'improvements', glass and furnishings, giving them a character that often speaks more of this period than their far longer histories.

Finally, it should be added that significant examples of twentieth-century church architecture are to be found (with the new Coventry Cathedral playing a pivotal role in the ecclesiastical design of the latter part of the century). It thus feels appropriate that some notable examples of modern twentieth-century architecture should be included on this list of Warwickshire's finest, a kind of journey through architectural history celebrating the diversity of styles and artistic expression to be found in England's centremost county.

The majority of the churches described in this book will generally be kept open to visitors, but a significant number are not and thus it is important to check before planning to visit a specific church, especially in the north of the county, where most either have limited openings or may require an appointment to see inside.

1. Alcester, St Nicholas

St Nicholas' makes a fitting visual climax to Alcester's High Street and has the grandeur befitting the main church of a small town. However, what may at first glance appear to be a genuine medieval church is soon revealed to be more of a hybrid, with the tall and stately west tower the only remaining part of the medieval building. The rest was rebuilt in the 1729–30 by Thomas Woodward of Chipping Campden with a strange fusion of a Gothic exterior (for its time a surprisingly considerate attempt to blend with the older tower) and fairly restrained baroque interior. Frederick Preedy rebuilt the chancel in 1870–71 and inserted the tracery in the nave windows, which gives the main body of the church a more Victorian appearance. Inside the nave retains its plain classical columns and flat plaster ceiling, the austerity relieved by a central chandelier suspended from a gilt cherub amid a ceiling rose of painted clouds.

This church is more remarkable for its monuments, most importantly the late Tudor tomb of Sir Fulke Greville and his wife in the north aisle from 1558 with recumbent effigies in painted alabaster and many children portrayed on the sides of the tomb-chest below. There is also a fine quality monument from 1828 by Sir Francis Chantrey to the 1st Marquis of Hertford in the south transept with a reclining effigy in white marble lying on a couch, while at the west end is a memorial to Sir Hamilton Seymour with a pensive seated marble statue by Count Gleichen dating from 1882. More unusual is the seventeenth-century Benefactors Board mounted on the wall of the north aisle, formed like a triptych with a framed parchment list flanked by hinged panels adorned with crude paintings of Acts of Charity in Jacobean costume.

The furnishings are mostly Victorian, but some tantalising fragments of what must have been the original late medieval rood screen remain affixed to the woodwork at the east end of the north aisle, which must have been an impressive piece when complete. The Victorian glass is limited to the chancel and west end with the remainder plain glazed, but happily there is a far more exciting modern window by Alan Younger (installed 1997) which enlivens the south aisle.

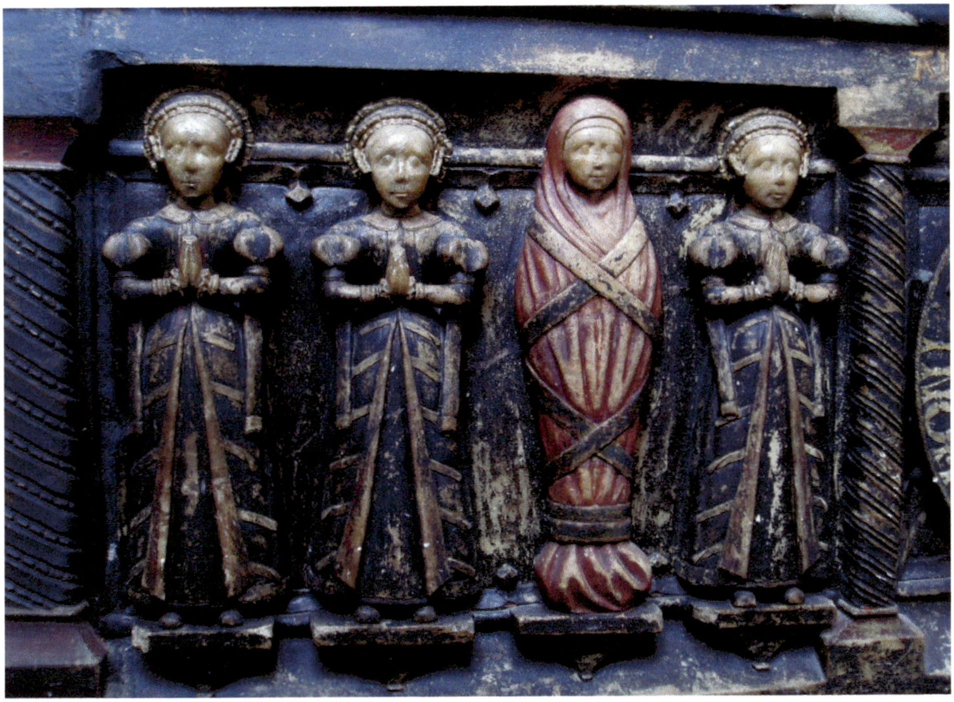

Some of the children of Fulke Greville, carved on his alabaster tomb from 1558, St Nicholas' Church, Alcester. The baby (represented at the same scale) denotes a child who died in infancy, a poignant reminder of child mortality that can be seen on most tombs of this period.

2. Ansley, St Laurence

One of the most handsome churches of north Warwickshire, St Laurence's stands in near isolation at Church End, some distance north-west of the modern village Ansley (the population having gravitated that way after the opening of the local colliery in 1874). The earliest parts of the present building are thought to date from *c.* 1050 and there are substantial Norman features such as the chancel arch (with sculpted capitals) and the north door. The soaring west tower is fifteenth century, as is much of the nave, while the chancel was extended eastwards in 1760 (its north window containing considerable fragments of medieval glass may be the former east window reused). The final addition was the north aisle and nave arcade of 1913.

Within the mixture of styles and dates is apparent as the eye is drawn towards the chancel, the altar sitting beyond a secondary arch further east since the eighteenth-century extension. A neat dark reredos takes the place of the usual east window (though a small oculus beyond it quirkily illuminates an IHS monogram pierced through its apex). The effect of the lengthened chancel from the nave is rather tunnel-like but pleasingly theatrical, the flanking Georgian memorials topped with urns adding to the sense of drama.

The most notable ancient feature is to be found on the left-hand side of the chancel arch, a curious carving of a small figure trapped between two beasts who

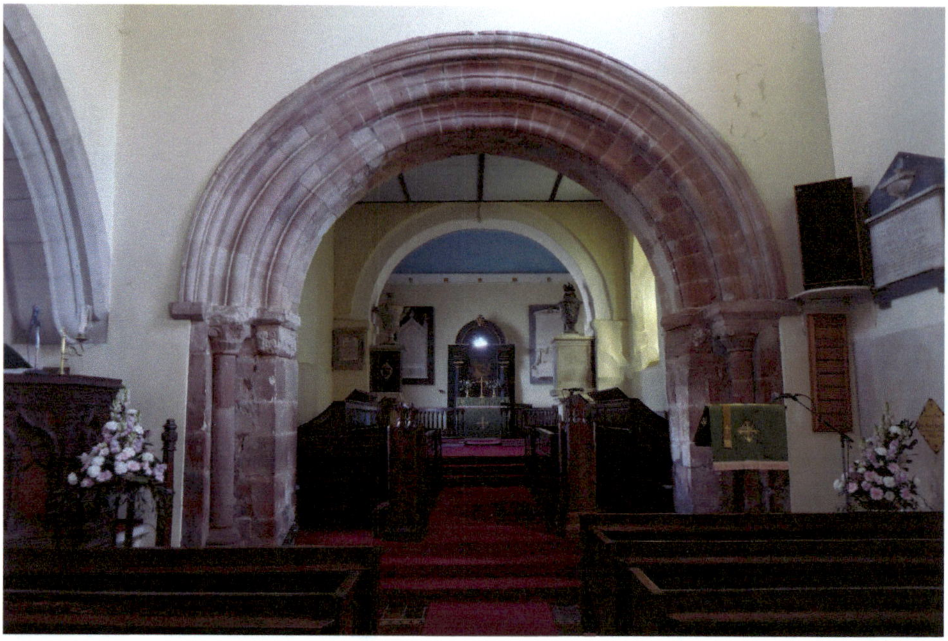

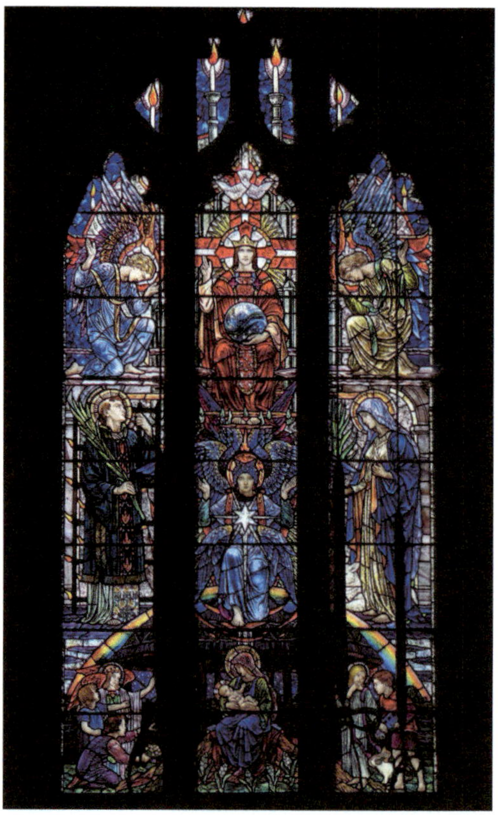

Above: The Norman chancel arch of St Laurence's Church, Ansley, the oldest part of the building. Beyond this is the Georgian sanctuary (the newest part), lit by a small oculus hidden behind the altar reredos.

Left: The dazzlingly rich Arts and Crafts west window in the tower, designed and made by Karl Parsons in 1931.

devour his arms (is this early Norman or late Saxon perhaps?). The north window of the sanctuary has substantial pieces of medieval glass relocated from elsewhere in the church; the left-hand light is an almost complete example of fourteenth-century decorative quarry glazing with a coat of arms at its centre, while balancing this is a fascinating patchwork of fifteenth-century fragments (including several heads and a small Virgin and Child). The real highlight of the church, however, is stained glass of much more recent date: the spectacular west window by Karl Parsons, one of the finest Arts and Crafts windows in existence. This dazzling display dates from 1931, and is a memorial to W. G. Phillips, great-grandfather of Captain Mark Phillips.

3. Astley, St Mary

Astley is barely even a village, a quiet rural settlement of just a few houses that nevertheless boasts a castle and one of the very finest and most rewarding churches in the county. The present church, impressive though it is, represents merely a fragment of what it once was, for it was originally founded as a collegiate church in 1343 by Sir Thomas Astley, and thus was built on a far more ambitious scale, more cathedral-like in dimensions than a normal parish church. It is incredible to think how imposing this great church in this tranquil spot must have been, when it was cruciform with a central tower crowned by a wooden spire (once known as the 'Lantern of Arden' while it was a major landmark). Following the dissolution of the college in 1545 it was abandoned and its materials plundered, its decline reaching a climax when the tower collapsed, demolishing much of the remaining nave and transepts below.

Salvation came a few years later in 1607 when Richard Chamberlaine decided to re-establish what remained of the building as a parish church, which entailed restoring the surviving fourteenth-century chancel and converting it into the nave of the present church. At the same time the present tower was built (most likely from recycled material from the ruins) on the site of the original, but now as the western termination rather than centre of the building. A new much smaller chancel was also built (in a style to complement the medieval work, a relatively rare example of Gothic Survival) by piercing a new chancel arch through the original east wall and its vast Perpendicular traceried window (which was blocked in but left visible inside and out). The church has remained remarkably little changed since this dramatic early seventeenth-century rebirth and the effect of its old and 'new' parts is surprisingly homogenous. This vast, splendid fragment of a church may have suffered immense losses, but what survives is more than satisfying, and it is astonishing to stand in its lofty 'nave' and try to imagine the additional volume of the lost original nave and transepts when this space was merely the chancel.

The most important features inside are the late fourteenth-century canopied choir stalls, which uniquely retain painted decoration in the form of a sequence of standing Apostles and prophets in the stall backs, with grapes and leaves above (the figures are of quite rustic quality but an amazingly complete survival nonetheless). Their scrolls were over-painted in English in 1624, but the original Latin text can still be made out underneath. The carved misericords below include

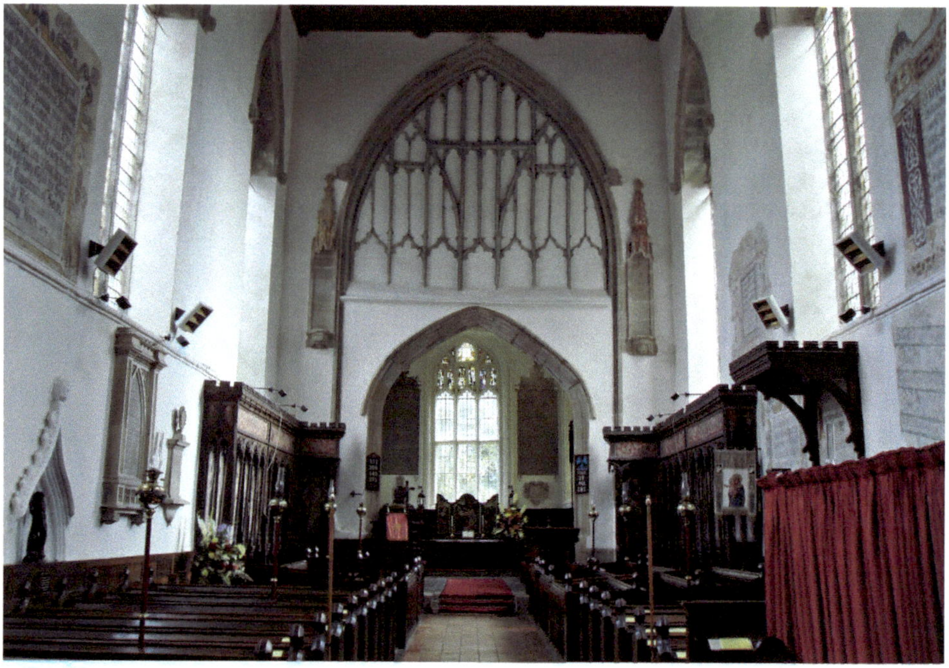

The present nave and former chancel of the original collegiate church, St Mary's, Astley. The old east window is blocked in with a new much smaller chancel added beyond in 1607.

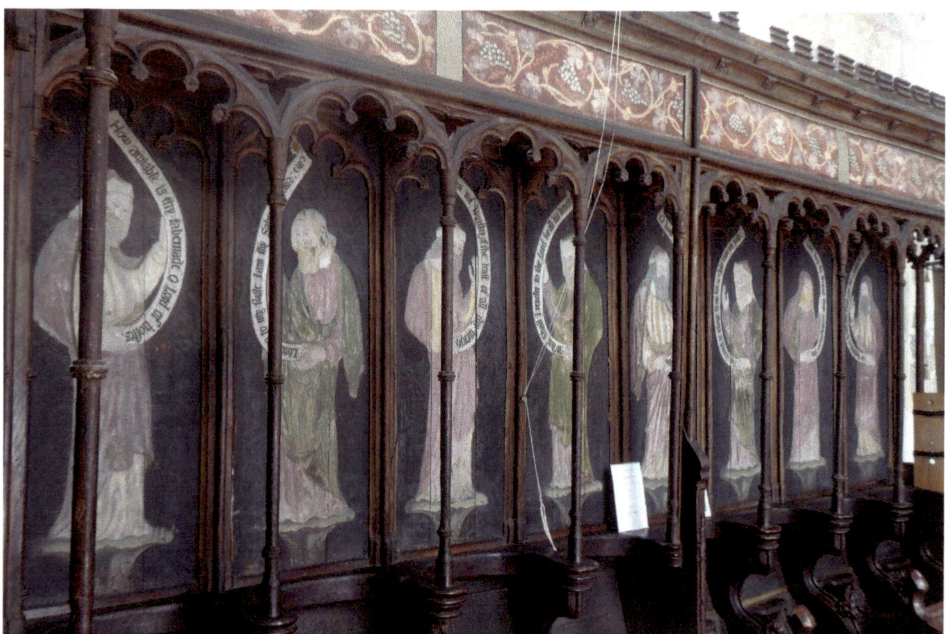

St Mary's late fourteenth-century choir stalls are a unique set, the backs adorned with painted figures holding scrolls: prophets on the south side (seen here) and Apostles to the north.

some lively heads and animals. How these stalls survived while the church was neglected after 1545 is unclear, but it is most fortunate that they were fit for reuse (repositioned further eastwards of their original site). They are of national significance, being such unique pieces, and yet rarely get the attention they deserve. There are also some good fragments of fourteenth-century glass in the north nave traceries and some later fragments in the present chancel too (a rare example of seventeenth-century reuse of medieval glass in a new building). At the west end are three late medieval alabaster effigies deposited on a single plinth, but originally from separate tombs elsewhere in the lost parts of the church; all commemorate members of Lady Jane Grey's family who owned the neighbouring castle from 1420 until 1554. The later features are noteworthy too, with the interior of the chancel especially charming, while the nave walls are enlivened with a series of ornamentally framed Biblical texts painted in *c.* 1610.

Just behind the church is Astley Castle, left ruined by neglect following fire damage in the 1980s but now refurbished as a popular Landmark Trust property in a strikingly successful synthesis of medieval and modern, with the ancient shell of the building clearly differentiated from the largely wooden contemporary structures within.

4. Aston Cantlow, St John the Baptist

This attractive church sits at the south-western edge of this pretty village and preserves several interesting features and retains an air of antiquity despite a restoration by William Butterfield in 1850 (which is most evident in the south wall of the nave which he rebuilt). Most of the building dates back to the thirteenth century, though the upper half of the west tower (featuring twin bell openings) is

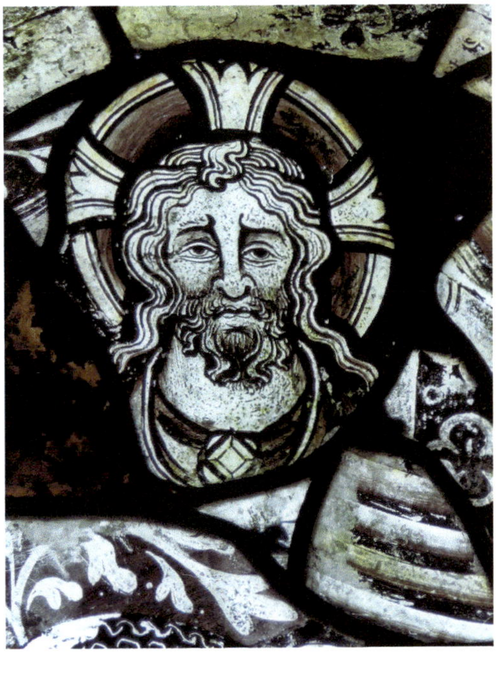

Early fourteenth-century head of Christ set amid fragments in a north aisle window of St John the Baptist's Church, Aston Cantlow, all that remains of the building's medieval glazing.

late medieval Perpendicular. The finest part of the building, architecturally, is the chancel which dates from the end of the thirteenth century and has a particularly fine group of early two-light traceried windows in the south wall (which leans outwards quite dramatically). There is a single aisle along the north side and above the north doorway is a niche containing a carving of the Nativity, but it is sadly weather-worn almost beyond recognition.

The interior is light and spacious and the eye is drawn eastwards to the fine late Victorian glass in the east window, which is by Charles Eamer Kempe from 1898, along with the smaller but prettier east window in the north aisle depicting the Adoration of the Magi from 1902. Two further windows are by O'Connor from the 1860s, while all that remains of the church's medieval glass are a few colourless fourteenth-century fragments at the head of two windows in the north aisle, including a particularly well-preserved head of Christ. There are a few examples of medieval woodwork remaining and an attractive late fifteenth-century font of a type found in several churches in the south of the county.

Aston Cantlow Church is thought by some to perhaps be where William Shakespeare's parents were married and his mother, Mary Arden, baptised. In more recent years, however, the church featured in national media after a legal battle over a chancel repair liability clause dating back to the reign of Henry VIII. The chancel has since been meticulously restored.

5. Baginton, St John the Baptist

Baginton today is somewhat squeezed between the outskirts of Coventry and its airport, which adjoins the village. It is, however, a place with a long history stretching back to Roman times, when a timber fort was established here known as The Lunt (parts of which were reconstructed in the 1970s). A castle was also built in Norman times and rebuilt in the fourteenth century, but sadly little more than foundations remain.

The somewhat elusive St John the Baptist's Church is at first sight a deceptively simple building, the view on approach from the south-east being that of a modest two-cell structure of nave and chancel with a miniature (and rustically charming) tower and spire perched between the two. Moving around to the opposite side, however, reveals that this building has undergone some extension, with no less than two north aisles. Much of the present building is still the original Norman one in essence, albeit with alterations and additions mostly of the fourteenth century. Everything is built in warm red sandstone, as is the norm in the central and northern parts of old Warwickshire.

The interior is quite different, both in terms of its whitened walls and unusual layout. From the west end the eye is drawn not to the usual single chancel arch, but three of them (technically six as the openings into the chancel beyond are set much lower). This configuration is necessitated by the two central piers being required to support the tiny box-like tower above, while the alcoves on either side may have once contained altars and retain significant patches of ancient wall painting (mainly floral decoration). It is difficult to get much sense of the small chancel beyond until passing through the arches, from where it is revealed as an intimate space full of interest.

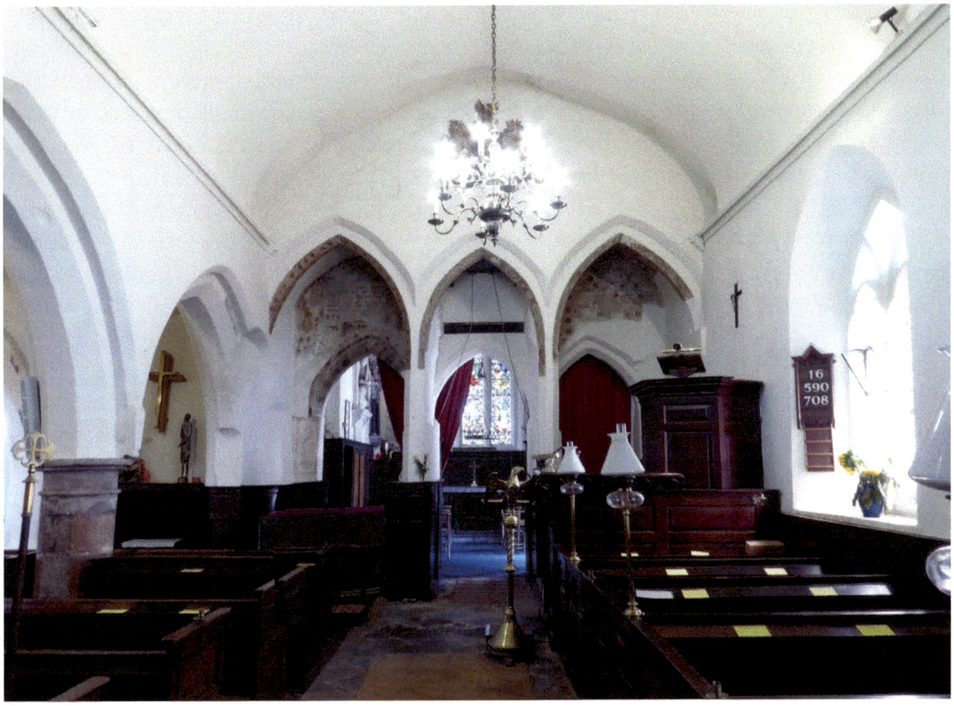

Above: View eastwards down the nave of St John the Baptist's Church, Baginton, towards the unusual triple-chancel arches, configured to carry the tiny bell tower above. Note the surviving patches of painted decoration.

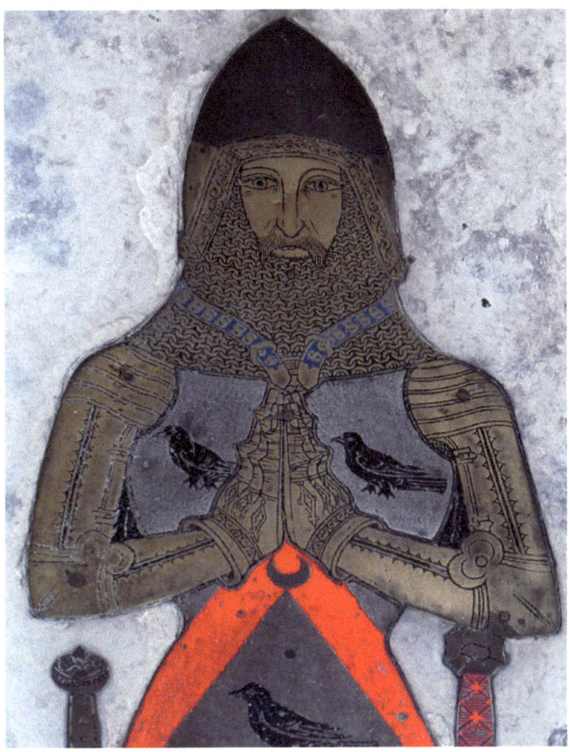

Right: Detail of the early fifteenth-century brass commemorating Sir William Bagot (d. 1407), now mounted to the wall of the chancel. The colouring was restored in the Victorian period.

The most noteworthy features of the church are to be found adorning the walls of the chancel, with several imposing eighteenth-century wall tablets (mostly to members of the Bromley family). However, the most important memorial here is a very fine early fifteenth-century brass commemorating Sir William Bagot (d. 1407) and his wife Margaret, who once lived in the nearby castle; the brass figures are unusual in featuring significant areas of colouring, though the polychrome appears to have been mostly restored in 1840. There are further patches of wall painting in other parts of the church and the nave retains most of its eighteenth-century furnishings. The Victorian restoration here happily appears to have had very little impact aside from the 1876 Hardman stained glass in the east window.

6. Barcheston, St Martin

Barcheston is a very secluded spot consisting of little more than the church and a couple of houses, and though very close to Shipston-on-Stour, it feels far more remote. The church is a delightfully picturesque building, originally a Norman structure modified in the thirteenth century, but its present appearance is largely the result of fifteenth-century remodelling. Its most distinguishing feature externally is the leaning north-west tower, which inclines dramatically to the west (where a mighty buttress adds reinforcement and blocks former windows) and has been thus nicknamed 'Warwickshire's Pisa'. The church's layout is somewhat irregular, the chancel slightly out of alignment with the nave and the south aisle more of a chapel extending only half the length. The north aisle has very domestic-looking post-medieval windows and an arcade that leans westwards as much as the tower does, amusingly propped up at this end by a corbel carved with a 'helping hand'.

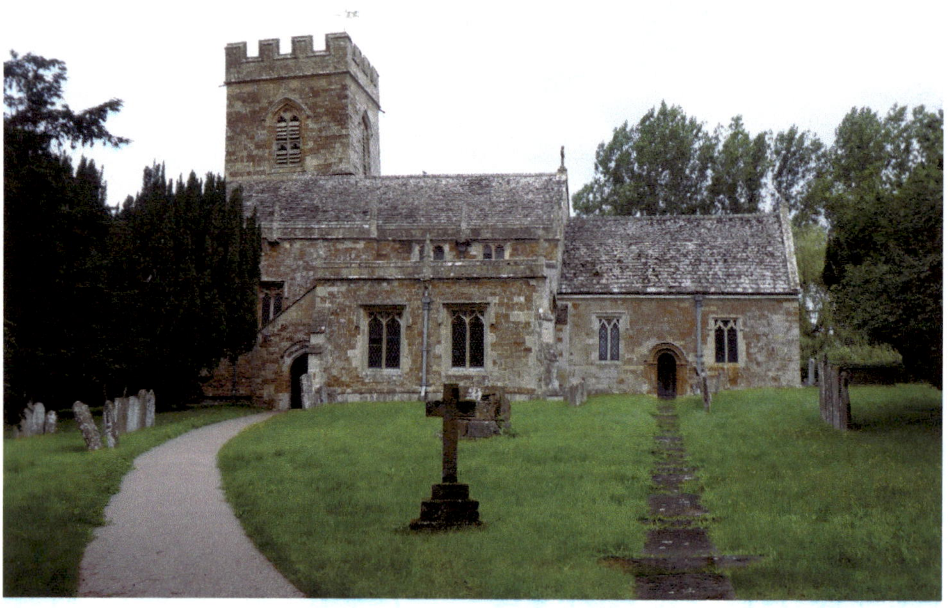

St Martin's Church, Barcheston, with its leaning tower tilting to the west, known affectionately as 'Warwickshire's Pisa'.

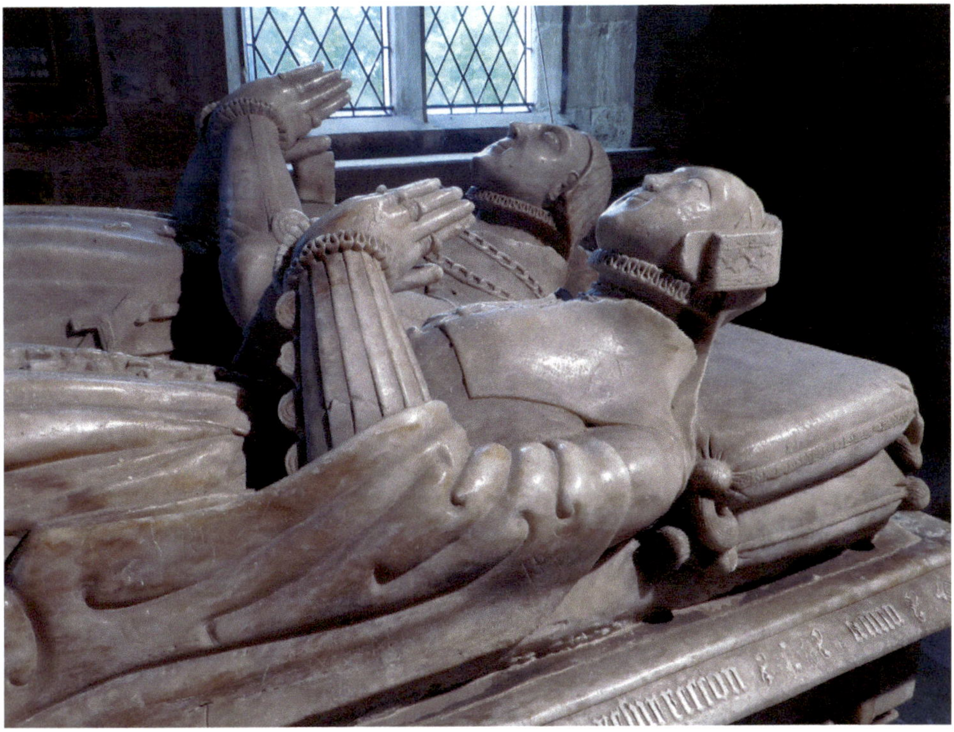

Alabaster tomb of William Willington and his wife, dating from 1555, medieval in spirit and Renaissance in detail.

The main items of interest here are the monuments in the south chapel, foremost being the Tudor tomb of William Willington (d. 1555) and his wife with effigies, believed to be the work of the Royley alabaster workshops of Burton-upon-Trent. The tomb is still very medieval in concept despite the Renaissance detail and costume, and is carved with the couple's children adorning the tomb-chest (consisting of seven daughters and six swaddled babes who died in infancy). Nearby is a tiny brass to former rector Hugh Humphray (d. 1530) set in a slab formerly in the chancel floor. Next to this is a large, incised slab to a layman of *c.* 1500, very worn and partially re-cut with a lozenge-shaped inscription to an eighteenth-century rector, ignominiously superimposed over the figure's legs! Above is a memorial tablet of 1675 unusually carved in wood.

The font is an attractive example of fourteenth-century Decorated style (though unfortunately rather green with damp). It was recently enhanced with a decorative glazed inner bowl by ceramicist Andrew Hazelden. The stained glass is largely Victorian work with the two most prominent windows by Hardman, but an intriguing fragment of eighteenth-century enamelled glass depicting the heads of two cherubs survives in the tracery of the south chancel window. The west window depicts the legend of St Martin dividing his cloak for the beggar, and is a late Arts and Crafts work of 1931 by Donald Brooke of Long Compton. The new organ cases recently installed happily frame the window without obscuring it.

7. Beaudesert, St Nicholas

St Nicholas' Church at Beaudesert sits unusually close to its neighbouring parish church, St John's in Henley, Arden – in fact, a mere hundred yards east of it. Each is clearly visible from the other, barely a stone's throw apart, separated only by a few houses and the narrow River Alne. It is the smaller of the two buildings, but architecturally and historically arguably the more important, with much of the present structure dating back to the Norman period, and still clearly evident in the structure of the chancel and the magnificent (if somewhat restored) south doorway.

The bulk of the building is in fact twelfth-century work except for the west tower, which is entirely fifteenth century Perpendicular and not fully aligned with the rest of the building. One of the most noticeable features is the way the chancel rises above the nave, to take into account the eastward slope of the churchyard. The east window has fine Norman chevron decoration similar to that of the south door.

Once inside, the richly decorated chancel arch is the real architectural showpiece of the interior, along with the contemporary chancel beyond it that has survived complete without later alteration other than a fourteenth-century window enlargement on the south side. The rib-vaulted ceiling, however, dates only to the 1864 restoration, but looks entirely at home with the original work (specifically the pilasters and corbels that support it which seem to have been designed to carry a structure like this), thus it appears that Victorian masonry has finally completed the original twelfth-century builder's vision (perhaps constrained by budget).

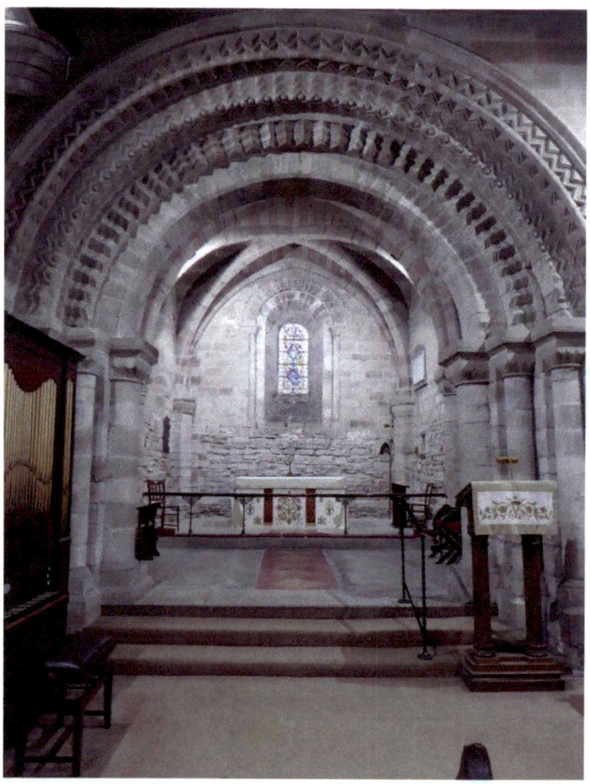

St Nicholas' Church, Beaudesert. The ornate Norman chancel arch with the vaulted chancel beyond, its ceiling a Victorian restoration but following the intentions of the twelfth-century builders.

The furnishings are mostly Victorian or later, save for a couple of simple fifteenth-century bench ends with coats of arms. The stained glass is entirely Victorian and, most importantly, includes some fairly early work by Morris & Co. dating from 1864 to 1865 which comprises the north and south windows of the nave. All these windows are quite restrained by their later standards with isolated figures on pale decorative backgrounds, deliberately light and subtle in palette to avoid darkening the interior. The figures are more Rossetti than Burne-Jones influenced (the norm in later years) and their individual designs supplied by several Pre-Raphaelite artists, namely Philip Webb, Ford Madox Brown, Edward Burne-Jones and even William Morris himself. It is a subtle scheme, but a satisfying one that has a far more benign impact on the church than the denser, more standard Victorian windows here.

8. Berkswell, St John the Baptist

There are few approaches to a church more memorable than a stroll into the churchyard at Berkswell, where one is confronted with one of the most picturesque views in Warwickshire. Immediately ahead is the rich-red-sandstone church (with its grey sandstone tower just peering over the rooftops) and a wonderfully complete Norman chancel, its east wall unusually intact with its charming group of small round-headed windows. The side walls also appear remarkably little altered (aside from a larger fourteenth-century window punctured through on the south side) and feature an intriguing row of primitive corbel heads under roof level. At the foot of the walls are windows, the first sign of this church's most surprising feature: a substantial Norman crypt! To enter one has to walk a little further up to a delightful timber-framed south porch, a wonder in itself.

The earliest parts of the present church represent the Norman rebuilding of the original Saxon church and comprises the crypt and chancel along with part of the north arcade of the nave, the rest of the nave and aisles being altered or expanded from the thirteenth century onwards, culminating in the addition of the squat but solid fifteenth-century tower. The wooden porch appears to be an early Tudor addition of *c.* 1500 and is surprisingly domestic in appearance with a room above, looking as if a small timber-framed cottage on stilts had been grafted on over the south doorway.

Entering the church through the south door initially reveals a rather confusing interior since the south aisle is still partitioned with a gallery above (now used as a chapel), thus the low ceiling comes as a surprise. Stepping into the nave the focus is the Norman chancel arch with what appears to be an old eighteenth-century reredos positioned above it. The wooden furnishings throughout the church are mainly early twentieth century and very attractive, though some eighteenth-century box pews remain at the west end. In the chancel are several fine late eighteenth- and early nineteenth-centuries sculpted marble memorials and early twentieth-century glass by Powell's in the Norman window openings.

The crypt is entered from the east end of the north aisle and is formed of two distinct chambers: one rectangular corresponding to the chancel above it, the other a curiously octagonal antechamber which sits under the east end of the nave but relates to little above. Both spaces are covered by ribbed stone vaults, borne on short pilasters with carved capitals, a degree of finish suggesting that the crypt was

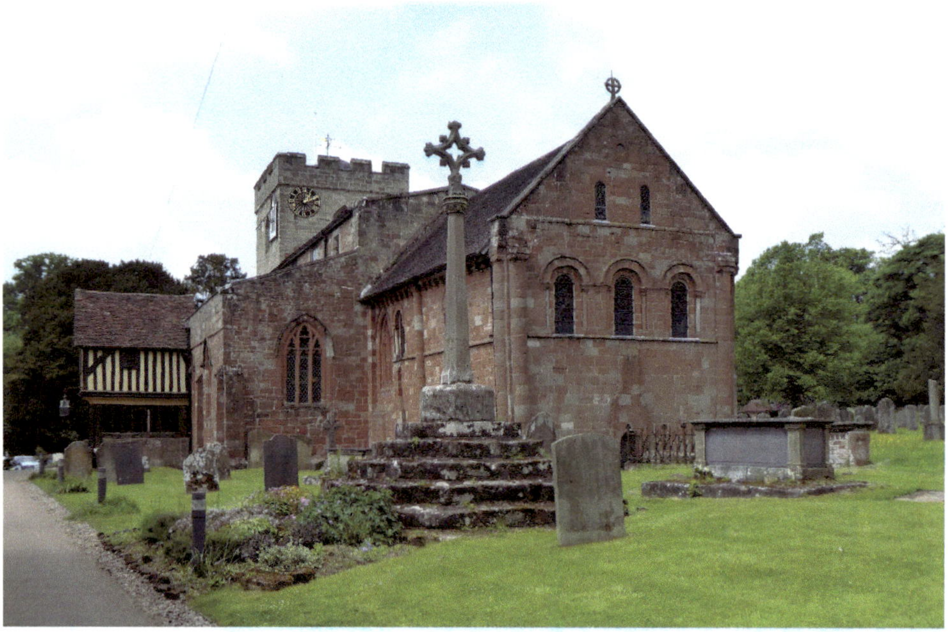

St John the Baptist's Church, Berkswell, as viewed from the east, showing the wonderfully complete Norman chancel and the delightful timber-framed porch.

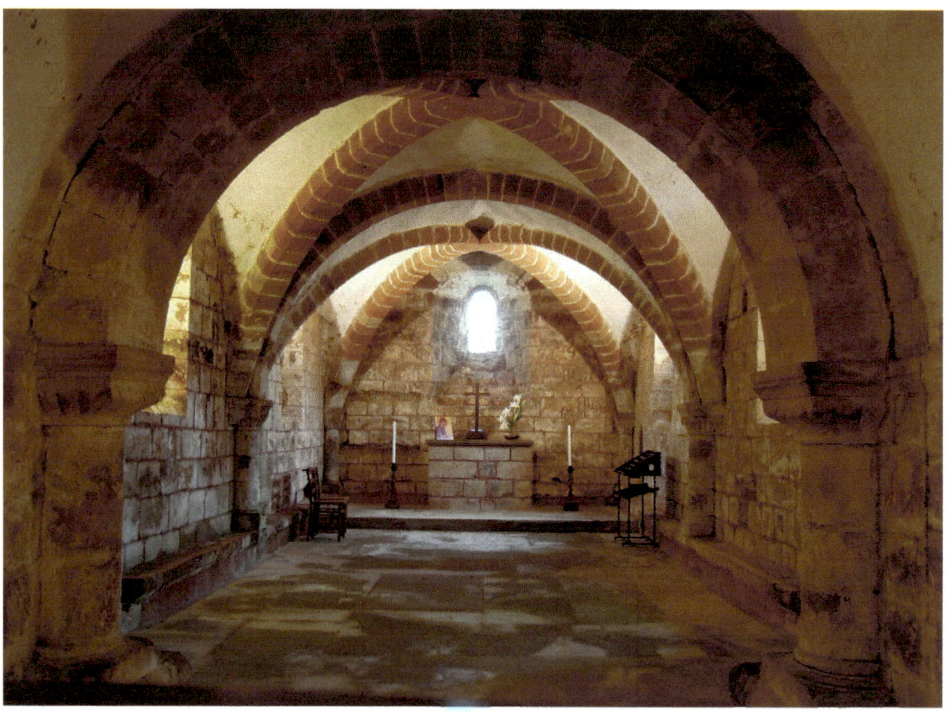

The eastern part of the Norman crypt beneath the chancel.

very much intended for use as a chapel or lower church. The octagonal antechamber now has a Victorian font at its centre to form a delightful baptistery, and the crypt remains cool at all times (refreshingly so if visiting on a hot summer's day).

Before leaving a couple of nearby landmarks deserve attention, most visibly the pretty Arts and Crafts Gothic structure of the 1921 war memorial at the eastern fringe of the churchyard. Opposite this, nearby is a stone-lined 16-ft-square pool, which is significant since the name Berkswell is reputedly derived from an Anglo-Saxon named Bercul, who either owned or was baptised in this well.

9. Billesley, All Saints

Billesley is a quiet, tiny settlement consisting largely of the old manor and the church, which is set back and largely hidden amid the trees of its small but lush churchyard. All Saints' Church is a petite building that at first sight appears to be an entirely seventeenth-century structure and, indeed, was rebuilt in 1692. However, while all the major features would seem to date from this period, they are clearly part of a remodelling of an earlier structure, and this small two-cell construction of an oblong nave and apsed chancel still embodies much of the Norman church.

The interior is regardless mostly a late seventeenth-century creation. Complete with its simple contemporary furnishings and box pews, it is a plain but refreshingly little altered space for Protestant worship untouched by the Victorians. The outstanding features here, however, are the pieces of twelfth-century sculpture housed in the small projecting south chapel or vestry. The smaller piece has a simple carving of the Harrowing of Hell with Christ rescuing a soul, though the

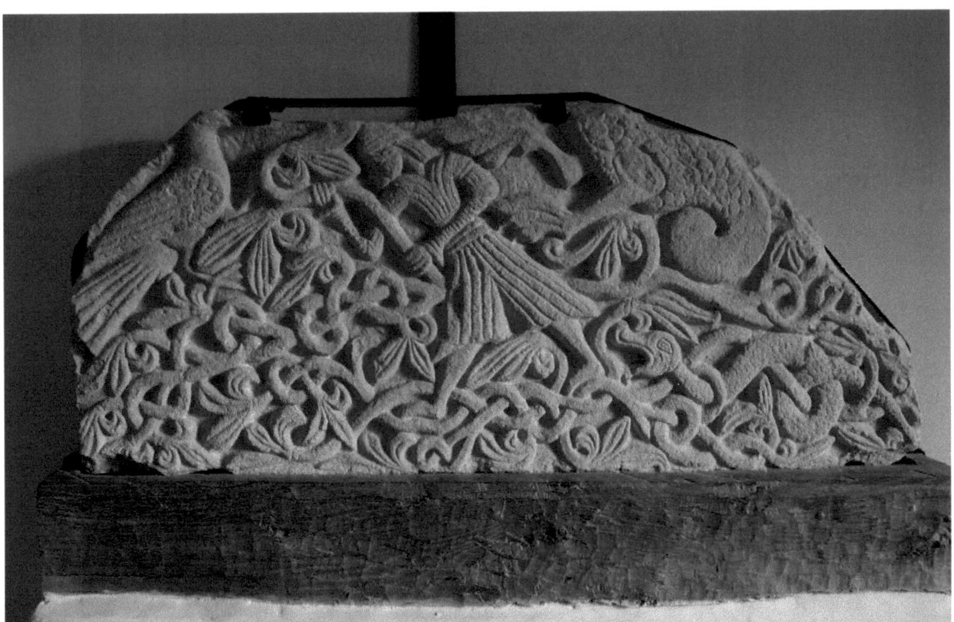

The Norman tympanum discovered in recent years at All Saints' Church, Billesley, depicting a man escaping the clutches of monstrous beasts.

sides of the block also have earlier Anglo-Saxon foliate carvings, suggesting a reuse by the Norman sculptor.

The larger piece is a finely carved tympanum, discovered in 1980 embedded in the wall under plaster. The carving is exuberant with much interlaced foliage and has been linked to the work of the renowned Herefordshire School of Romanesque sculpture. Its subject is rather vague, depicting a man in profile escaping harassment by a serpent and a (now headless) dragon moving towards a bird on the left, suggesting an escape from evil forces. It was briefly displayed in London in 1984 as part of an excellent exhibition of English Romanesque art.

The church is no longer used for services and has been vested in the Churches Conservation Trust; it is normally kept locked, but a key is usually available from the neighbouring hotel.

10. Brailes, St George

Brailes is one of the more picturesque villages of south Warwickshire, and in medieval times was a larger settlement and thriving centre of the wool trade. The church of St George reflects this, being justly renowned as one of the county's grandest parish churches. It is an impressively large building of attractively golden-brown ironstone, begun in the late thirteenth century but dating mainly from 1325–75, and terminated by a very lofty west tower (finished in the following century), a handsome edifice that announces the church's presence from afar. The rest of the exterior is initially harder to appreciate given the cramped nature of the churchyard on the south side, though its details can be enjoyed, such as the pretty fifteenth-century parapet above a frieze of carved heads and elements of foliage that enrich the south side. The spiky Sanctus-bell turret is a pleasing

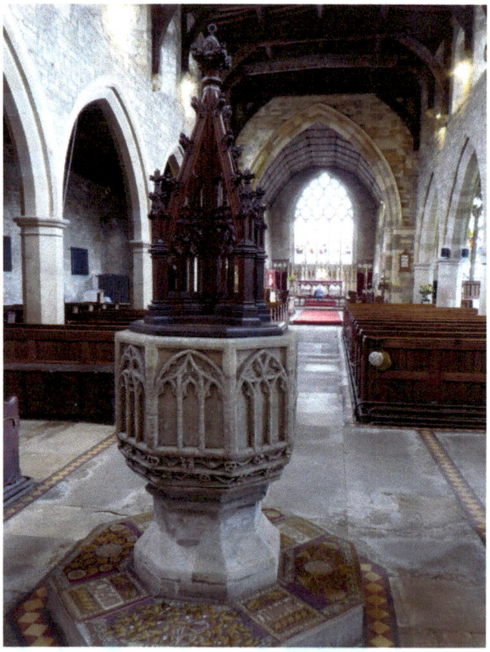

The nave of St George's Church, Brailes, with its fine fourteenth-century font, featuring designs like traceried windows.

feature marking the junction of nave and chancel, though only dates from the thorough restoration of the church, 1877–79.

The main body of the church impresses more with its substantial length and width than height, and is entered by a substantial porch on the south side. Once inside the great sense of space punctuated by arches and columns is impossible to ignore; the wooden roof above seems to stretch forever onwards and is supported by some amusingly carved human and animal head-corbels. As happened so often the Victorian restorers scraped the walls of their plaster back to the stonework and then began the process of filling the windows with a mixed collection of stained glass, so the level of lighting is somewhat subdued. The large east and west windows are rather uninspiring pieces in earthy tones by Ward & Hughes, but some of the later glass is better, particularly the rich Ruth & Naomi window by William Glasby (follower of Henry Holiday) in the north aisle dating from 1925.

A fine fourteenth-century font stands at the west end carved with geometric designs like traceried windows, differing on each side is if based on pages from some medieval mason's pattern-book. In the south aisle is a very heavily eroded medieval priest's effigy on a tomb-chest, worn beyond recognition, its condition explained by the fact it originally stood in the churchyard until being brought inside to protect it from further weathering only in 1933. Nearby is a plain seventeenth-century tomb-chest in black marble with a tablet to Richard Davies crowned with a carved stack of books.

Brailes, SS Peter and Paul

Not far away in Friars Lane is the Roman Catholic church of St Peter and St Paul, unusual in having been converted from the upper floor of a medieval barn (later used as a malthouse) attached to the side of the former Rectory Farm. The chapel

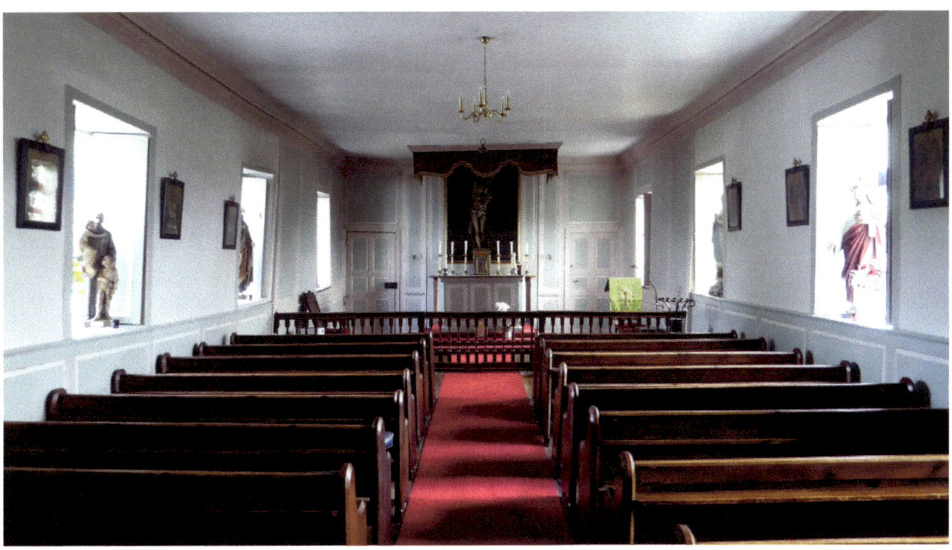

St Peter and St Paul's Roman Catholic Church, Brailes, a rare example of a hidden recusant chapel still in use.

was created in 1726 as a secret recusant church (predating Catholic Emancipation by a century), thus the completely domestic exterior gives nothing away. Only when one ascends a staircase to the right of the main door of the adjacent house does one encounter the extraordinary eighteenth-century church complete with its original fittings and painted altarpiece of the Crucifixion. Stained-glass panels of Catholic martyrs (from the closed RC chapel in Ilmington) were installed in the north-facing windows in 2025. As a reminder of less tolerant times, it is a rare survival and a little-known gem.

11. Burton Dassett, All Saints

Set in a delightful churchyard on the slopes of the Dassett Hills is one of Warwickshire's most picturesque churches, surrounded by beautiful countryside but curiously no village. The settlement here suffered two cruel blows: the Black Death of 1348–49 and enclosure under an unscrupulous landowner in *c.* 1500, both resulting in depopulation and the rather isolated church we see today.

The church is built from beautifully toned ironstone and surprisingly grand for such a remote spot, the chancel rising to the east to accommodate the hillside contours. Little remains of the Norman period beyond the north doorway; most of what we see today is of the thirteenth-century rebuilding and expansion giving the nave aisles and transepts on both sides, the final addition being the square fourteenth-century tower at the west end.

Within, the church is a delight, its bright whitewashed interior showing no sign of Victorian intervention (it was restored in 1880 but happily imperceptibly and

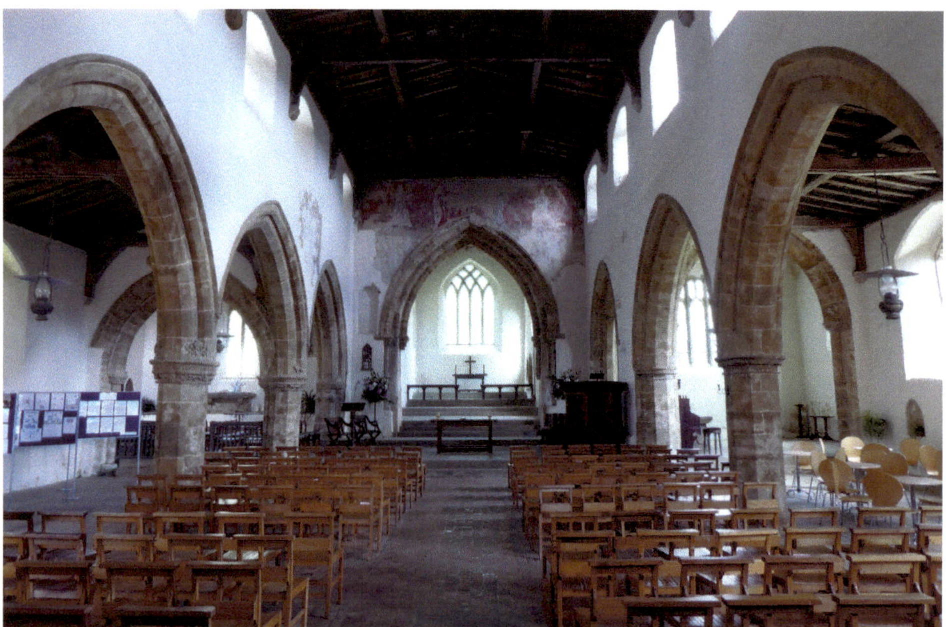

All Saints' Church, Burton Dassett, has a delightful interior. Of particular interest are the well-preserved medieval wall paintings above the chancel arch and some lively carved capitals in the north side.

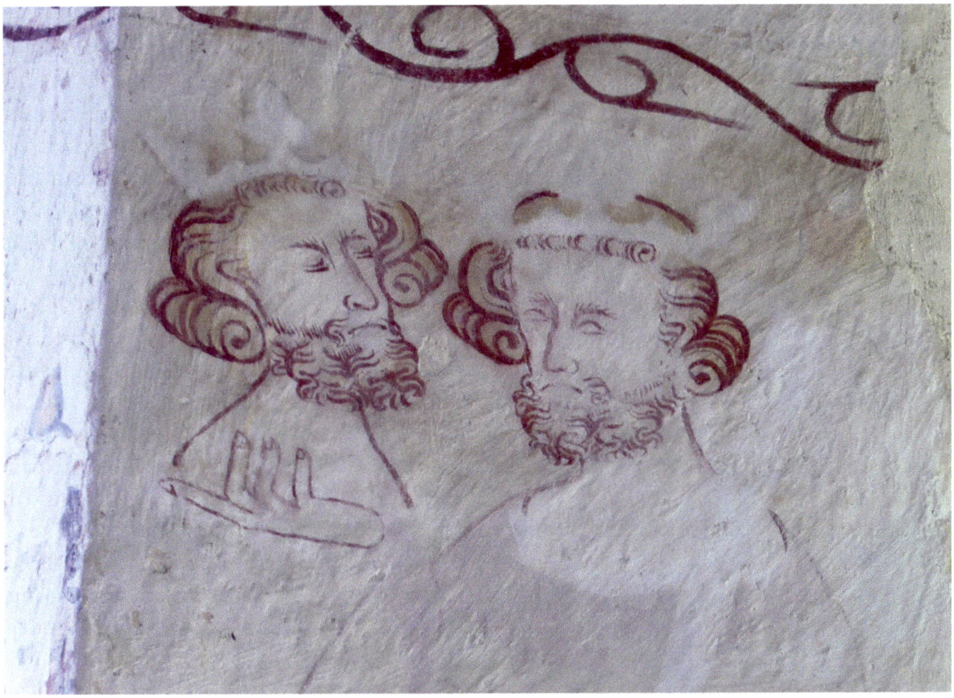

Fourteenth-century painted figure of a king holding a head that appears to be a mirror image of his own.

thus retains its character). The features that draw the eye most are the wonderful carved capitals of the north nave arcade dating from *c.* 1290: alive with various beasts, many chasing each other amid swirling foliage – a very memorable display. The other main notable features are the surviving fragments of wall painting, including a well-preserved section over the chancel arch depicting Mary and St John with angels flanking the (now lost) Cross against a vibrant red background. This appears to have been painted in the late fourteenth century over a Last Judgement from a century earlier (parts of which are still visible below) and was probably done to complement the long since lost rood screen. Further fragments of thirteenth-century mural decoration can be seen in the window reveals of the north transept, most notably the two figures of kings, one of whom examines a crowned severed head. There are also pieces of post-Reformation decoration here and in the nave.

12. Charlecote, St Leonard

St Leonard's Church is situated by the main entrance to Charlecote Park and contains sixteenth- and seventeenth-century monuments to its builders and residents, the Lucy family, in the north chapel. The medieval church has gone and what we see now is an entirely Victorian building dating from 1851 to 1853 designed by John Gibson. It is a flamboyant exercise in Victorian Gothic with lavish details and some French inspiration in the slender steeple and exuberant rose window at the west end.

The interior is somewhat dark due to a full scheme of Victorian glass and, unusually, the entire length of nave and chancel is finished with a stone-vaulted ceiling – another reminder that generous funding was available for this building. The furnishings are all of a piece with the architecture, as is most of the glass (mostly of the 1850s with two later windows by Kempe).

The Lucy Chapel on the north side is the main point of interest here, containing three imposing monuments relocated from the old church. Each commemorates a different Sir Thomas Lucy and his wife, and all bear their effigies. The first two are of alabaster from the 1600s, straddling the end of Elizabeth's reign and the accession of James I; the earlier Sir Thomas (d. 1600) lies with his wife on a tomb-chest against the east wall, while the next (d. 1605) has a far more ostentatious superstructure around Sir Thomas's effigy with his wife kneeling before him. The final Lucy monument is the finest; Sir Thomas (d. 1640) has a splendid tomb in white marble beneath a canopy borne on black marble columns. It was commissioned from the finest sculptor of its time, Nicholas Stone, though much of the actual carving was done by an accomplished assistant. Their effigies are of the highest quality. She lies in the foreground, he is a little higher resting on his elbow, and behind him a carved bookcase with the titles 'Homer, Horace, Virgil, Cato, Xenophon, Winter's Ayres' – clearly the deceased wished to be remembered as a man of learning!

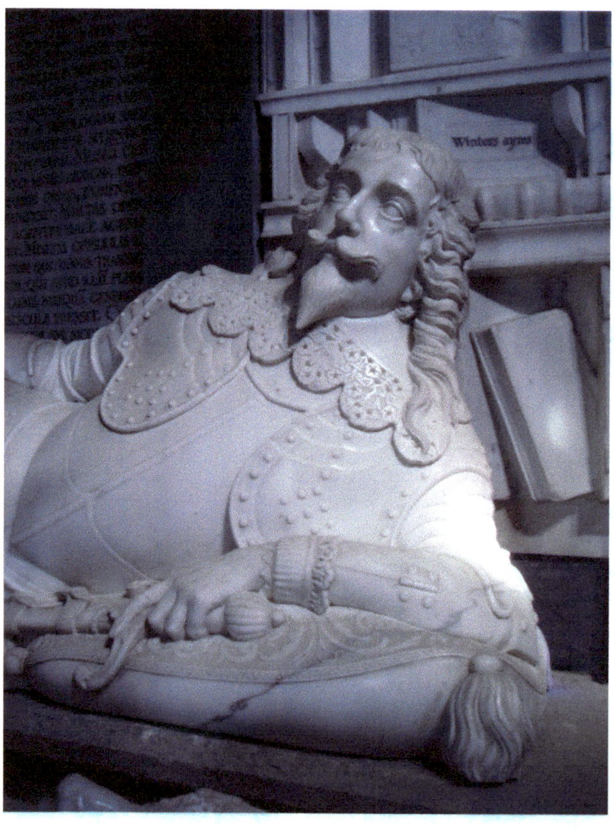

Marble effigy of Sir Thomas Lucy (d. 1640) from his tomb at St Leonard's Church, Charlecote, on the north side of the Lucy Chapel, by Nicholas Stone and his assistants.

13. Cherington, St John the Baptist

Cherington is a picturesque south Warwickshire village that feels and looks close to the Cotswolds. Its church is an attractive edifice dating mainly from the thirteenth to fifteenth centuries and announces its presence from afar with a handsome west tower. The rest consists of chancel and nave with a single aisle on the north side. The south wall was raised to incorporate a row of clerestory windows in the late medieval period, a common practice at this time to increase the amount of light within.

Inside the nave and north aisle are pleasantly light with their whitewashed walls, while the chancel is a darker, more mysterious space beyond. The most striking feature when looking down the nave is the elegant, canopied tomb of a fourteenth-century civilian that interrupts the eastern end of the arcade. The identity of the hooded man whose effigy lies under the almost flattened cusped ogee arch is unknown, but he was clearly a local landowner of some importance. The tomb-chest below is unusual in incorporating a piscina basin on its north side to serve an adjacent altar.

The other outstanding feature here is the glass, an astonishing collection of antiquarian pieces gathered from various unknown sources by Revd John Warner, rector 1741–80. There are many fascinating fragments of stained glass of various dates, styles and origins. Some windows are arranged as a sequence of largely heraldic medallions, while others contain intriguing assemblages of figurative fragments, the best being the collection of random elements in the east window of

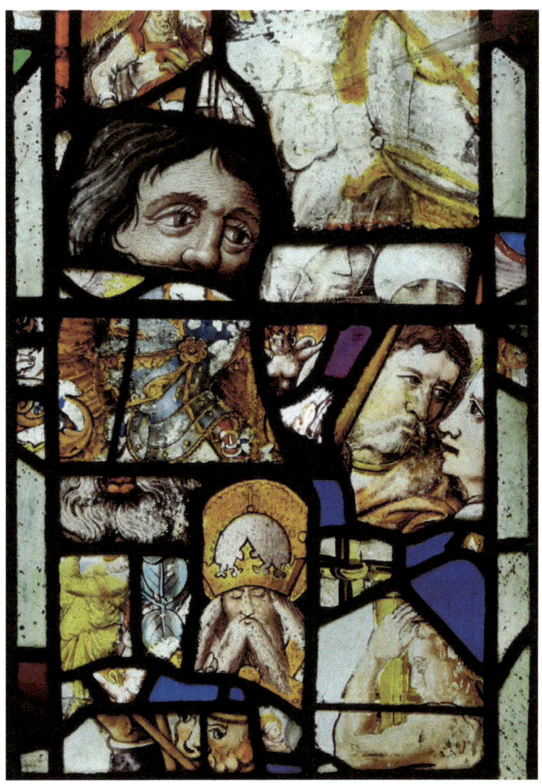

An interesting assemblage of largely mid-sixteenth-century Continental fragments in the south-west window of the nave, St John the Baptist's Church, Cherington.

the north aisle (including a fourteenth-century St John and an eighteenth-century enamelled head of Christ) and the westernmost window in the south wall of the nave with its fascinating collage of fragments of mainly sixteenth-century date (mostly Continental). There is something of interest in nearly every window here, which makes a visit to this church especially memorable.

14. Chesterton, St Giles

Chesterton feels far more remote than it should, an ancient settlement but now a ghost of its former self with a mere scattering of houses and the church. It is best known for its seventeenth-century windmill on a hilltop nearly a mile to the north-west. Originally there was a great mansion here immediately north of the churchyard, but this was demolished in 1802, leaving only a lone brick archway standing as a handsome but eerie reminder, framing the emptiness beyond.

The church is a long, low building without aisles, mostly dating from the fourteenth and fifteenth centuries but earlier in origin. The squat west tower is an early seventeenth-century addition and the chancel (structurally continuous with the nave) was much altered in the Victorian period. The best features externally are the south doorway (with fourteenth-century ball-flower decoration) within the porch, while above this is a curious early fifteenth-century carving depicting the Three Magi under canopies, presumably a fragment of a former altar reredos.

The interior has a tunnel-like effect, being one long chamber without aisles under a late medieval timber roof, the chancel separated only by a modest screen. It is most memorable for the group of monuments at the west end of the nave,

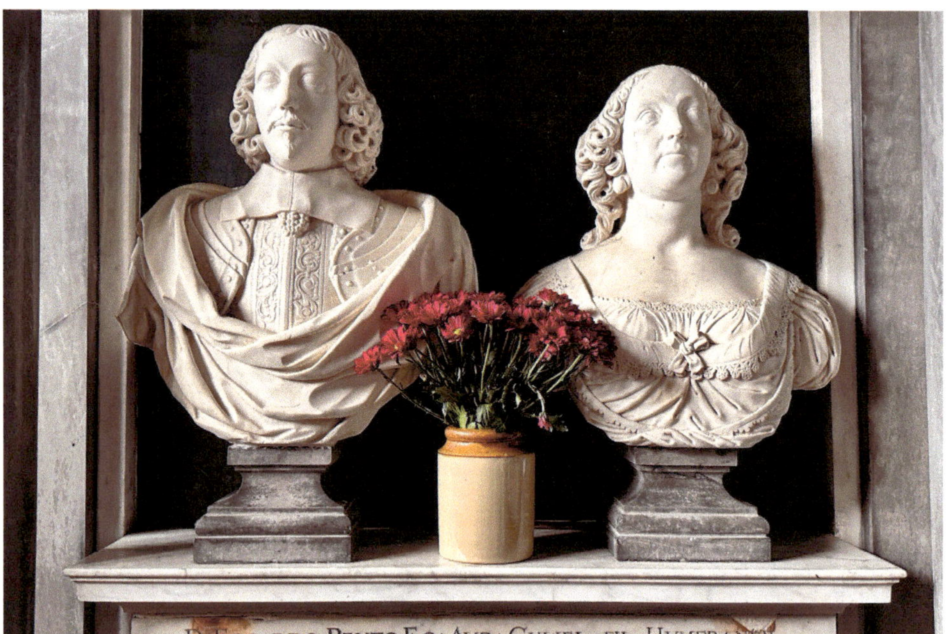

St Giles' Church, Chesterton. Busts from the monument to Edward Peyto and his wife Elizabeth, carved by John Stone, 1643.

all to members of the Peyto family, builders of the renowned nearby windmill and former occupants of the now vanished mansion. The largest monument is to Humphrey Peyto (d. 1585) and is of alabaster with effigies of the deceased couple in Elizabethan fashion and ten children depicted in relief behind them. Of much higher quality are the two marble monuments with busts to Sir William Peyto (d. 1609) and his son Sir Edward (d. 1643) with their wives, the work of Nicholas Stone and his son, John Stone, respectively.

15. Cheylesmore, Christ Church

Now for something a little different, a church that is often described as embodying the 'Festival of Britain' style and spirit, and this is no exaggeration. Situated in the southern suburbs of Coventry, Christ Church was built in 1954–57 on an ambitious scale to replace the war-damaged Christ Church in the city centre (a Victorian rebuilding of the medieval Greyfriars church, of which only the octagonal steeple remains, the third of Coventry's famous 'Three Spires'). Designed by A. H. Gardner & Partners, this was one of the grandest and most expensive post-war churches in the country, and says much about the vision and optimism with which new churches were constructed at the time.

The church takes the form of a vast triple-aisled hall, the roof forming a low curve over each aisle which gives the main façade, with its largely glazed walls, a distinctive outline. Next to this rises the tapering oblong tower with its curious chequerboard top storey (originally a mixture of glazed panels and louvered grills, but replaced by brickwork in more recent years).

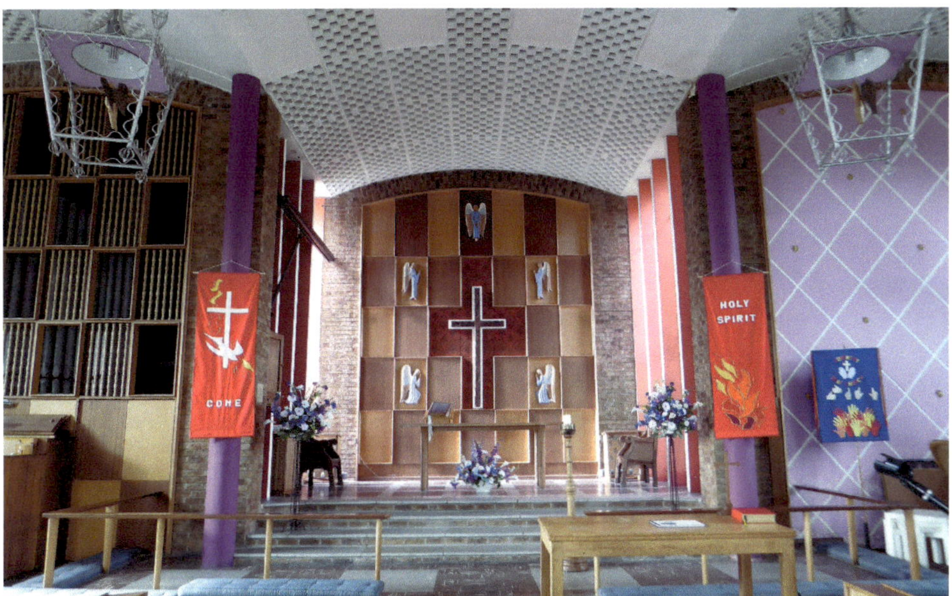

The altar area at Christ Church, Cheylesmore, illustrating the use of contrasting material and colouring in this fine 'Festival of Britain'-style church. Note the curious lamp fittings with small angels caged like canaries.

The interior is the most astonishing sight here: a great open space only lightly divided into three aisles by slender concrete columns, supporting a great expanse of concave plaster ceiling above, replete with perforated panels (decorated with badges of city guilds). The expanses of brick and woodwork are relieved by an unusually bold colour scheme of purple columns and a pinkish lilac for wall panelling (again with a chequered configuration on the south side). Each aisle terminates in a decorative wall finish, most notably the chancel with its wooden reredos with carved angels by John Skelton, whose Evangelist figures also adorn the nearby pulpit. Further angels can be found in more surprising places, a pair flank a clock above the tower door, but most eccentric of all are the tiny wooden figurines suspended in oddly birdcage-like light-fittings along the nave, giving these angels the appearance of caged canaries!

The vast windows are mostly of textured glass, but each contains a pair of densely coloured *dalle-de-verre* stained-glass panels, figurative images from the Life of Christ by Pierre Fourmaintraux from 1955. These mosaics of glass chunks set in concrete are very rich, but, alas, overwhelmed by the clear glass surrounding them. Nevertheless, they form a rare scheme in this medium, and illustrate the unusual degree of artistry lavished on this church.

Coundon, St George

For an interesting contrast and lesson in modern church architecture, nearby St George's Church at Coundon (a western Coventry suburb) should be compared as an equally bold vision of modern church architecture but from a pre-war perspective, a mere two decades earlier. Built in 1938 to the designs

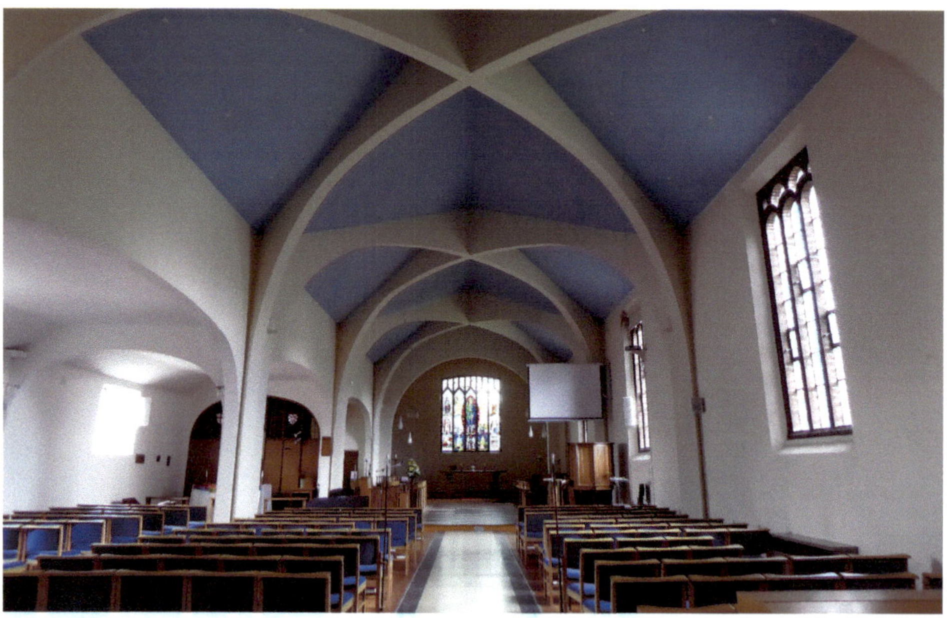

St George's Church, Coundon. A fine pre-war church by N. F. Cachemaille Day, its nave covered with a strikingly modern reinterpretation of a medieval vaulted ceiling.

of N. F. Cachemaile-Day, this is a smaller more Gothic influenced structure, though interpreted with more severity than delicacy in solid masses of brick and distinguished externally by a squat yet muscular square tower rising to an octagon crowned by a slate-covered spire. The real treat here is the striking interior with its concrete ribbed vault, evoking the medieval spirit but totally modern in form. There is an impressive octagonal baptistery beneath the tower with a tapering font cover, and fetching figurative glass by W.T. Carter Shapland from 1965 in the east window.

16. Coleshill, SS Peter and Paul

This market town church is dominated by its splendid steeple, a landmark for miles around and similar to those of other prosperous Midland red-sandstone churches (particularly King's Norton which is a virtual twin). It is a large, mainly fourteenth to fifteenth century building which has undergone significant Victorian restoration (most external detail was renewed owing to the soft red sandstone) but remains a grand medieval church full of interest.

The nave is rather long and cavernous but is followed by a lighter Perpendicular chancel with large windows (filled with Victorian glass by Clayton & Bell).

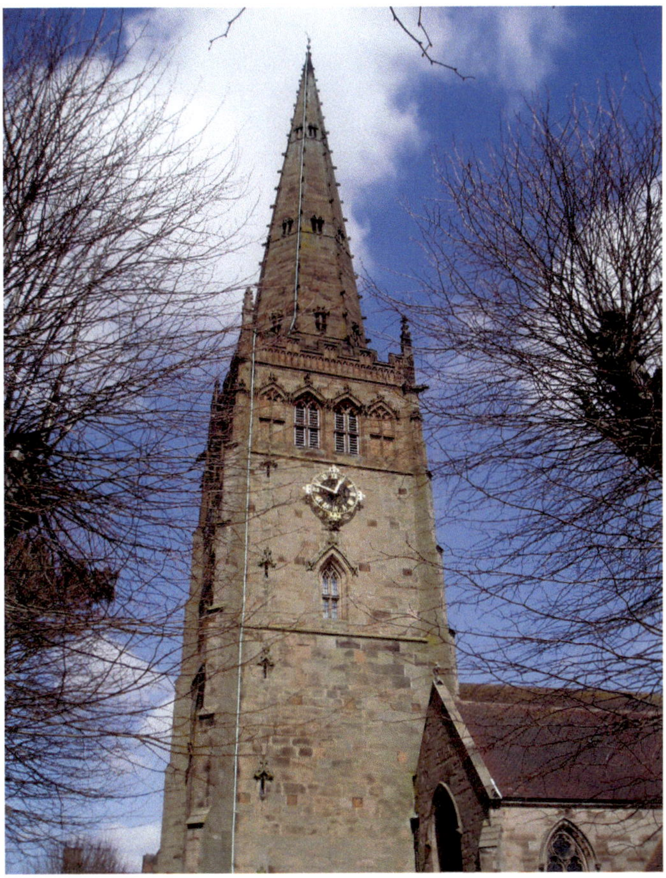

The handsome west tower and spire of SS Peter and Paul's Church, Coleshill, which is almost identical to the contemporary steeple at Kings Norton, thus presumably the work of the same masons.

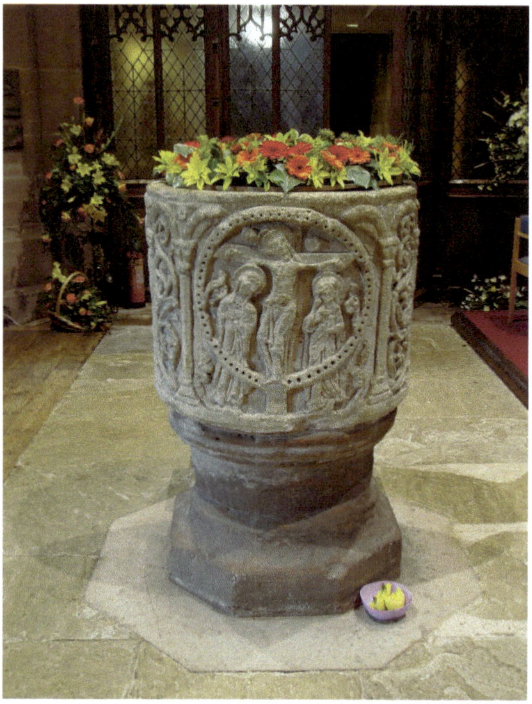

The superb twelfth-century Norman font, with a depiction of the Crucifixion on its eastern side.

The oldest treasure here is the Norman font, unusually adorned with a Crucifixion and four saints in relief amid curling foliage, much worn by time but still enjoyable.

The other main reason to visit this church is its impressive collection of monumental tombs with effigies, the earliest being two thirteenth century knights, one under a recess in each aisle, but the rest are concentrated in the chancel which feels more like a mausoleum for members of the Digby family. There are three large Tudor tombs with effigies of the deceased couples (two stylistically late medieval, the other very much Elizabethan) and a further late medieval tomb-chest crowned by an incised slab. There are a couple of small priest's brasses in the floor and more Digby memorials, including a large seventeenth-century urn.

17. Compton Verney, Chapel

Most visitors come to admire the superb Verney mansion, now restored as an art gallery and popular visitor attraction set in a beautiful park. Most will likely be unaware of the chapel, hidden as it is from view behind the stately home; indeed, it has only in recent years been restored and reopened to the public.

The medieval village east of the lake had become depopulated by 1500 and nothing now remains. The ancient church was situated nearby but demolished in 1772 (apparently to improve the view from the house) and its replacement next to the house built in 1776–79 to the designs of Capability Brown. It is a simple rectangular building with arched windows, externally a little severe but internally a beautifully light space with gleaming white walls and furnishings, a wonderfully unspoilt period-piece eighteenth-century interior.

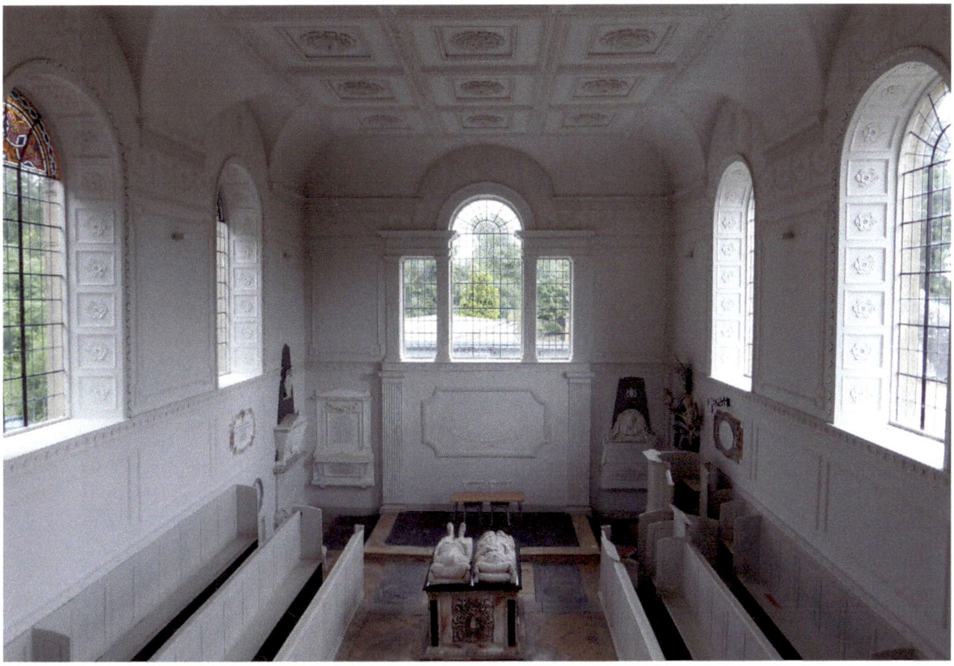

Interior view of the 1770s chapel at Compton Verney designed by Capability Brown, as viewed from the west gallery.

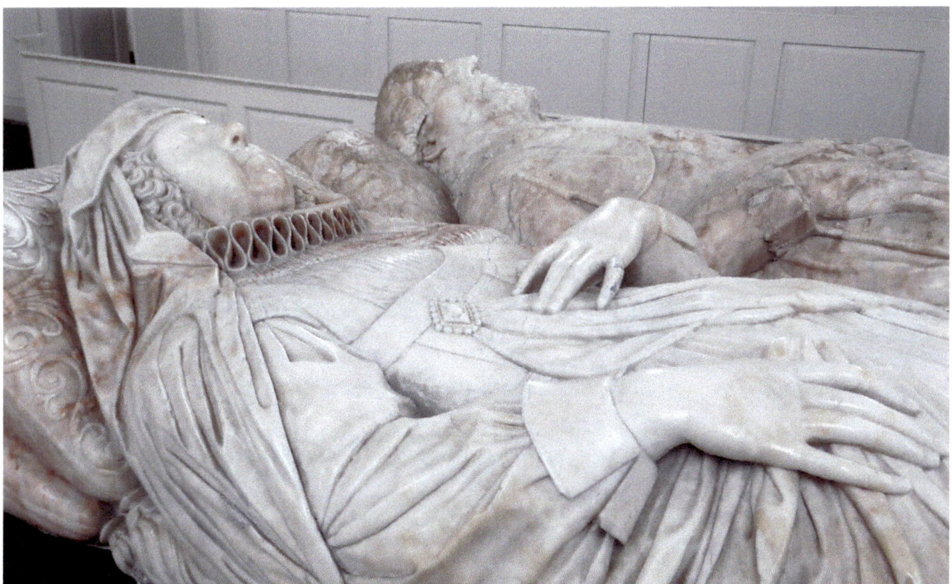

Tomb with effigies of Sir Richard Verney (d. 1630) and his wife Margaret, carved by Nicholas Stone.

Of special interest are the monuments, the best having been relocated from the old church. Earliest are the Tudor brasses in the floor, but most imposing is the centrally positioned tomb of Sir Richard Verney (d. 1630) and his wife Margaret with white marble effigies by Nicholas Stone. More exuberant perhaps is the fully baroque monument in black and white marble nearby to Sir Greville Verney (d. 1668) with a periwigged bust attributed to Caius Gabriel Cibber.

18. Coughton, SS Peter and Paul

Coughton is a real treat for the church crawler. Not only is its fine medieval church situated next to the impressive façade of Coughton Court, it also has an attractive Victorian RC church as its neighbour to the south (built for the Court's owners, the Throckmortons, who, being Catholic, required another church). St Peter's is easily one of the most rewarding churches in the area, a late medieval building with much of interest within. Most of what we see today was rebuilt in Perpendicular style by Sir Robert Throckmorton between 1486 and 1518 and has a pleasing uniformity. The chancel was provided with ample side chapels considerably wider than the adjacent nave aisles.

Within, the church is light and pleasant and one soon notices the cenotaph of its builder, Sir Robert (d. 1518), given due prominence in the centre of the nave (since he died in the Holy Land it is actually occupied by a later Sir Robert). Like most of the tombs here, it is a simple tomb-chest without an effigy, the rest being located

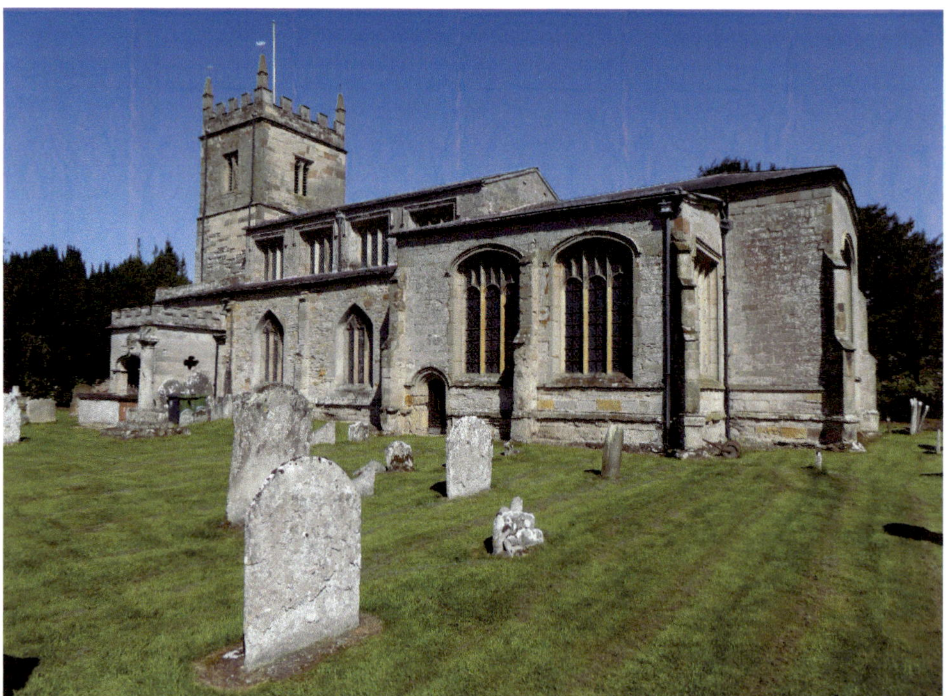

SS Peter and Paul's at Coughton is a good example of a late medieval estate church, rebuilt in Perpendicular style by Sir Robert Throckmorton in 1486–1518.

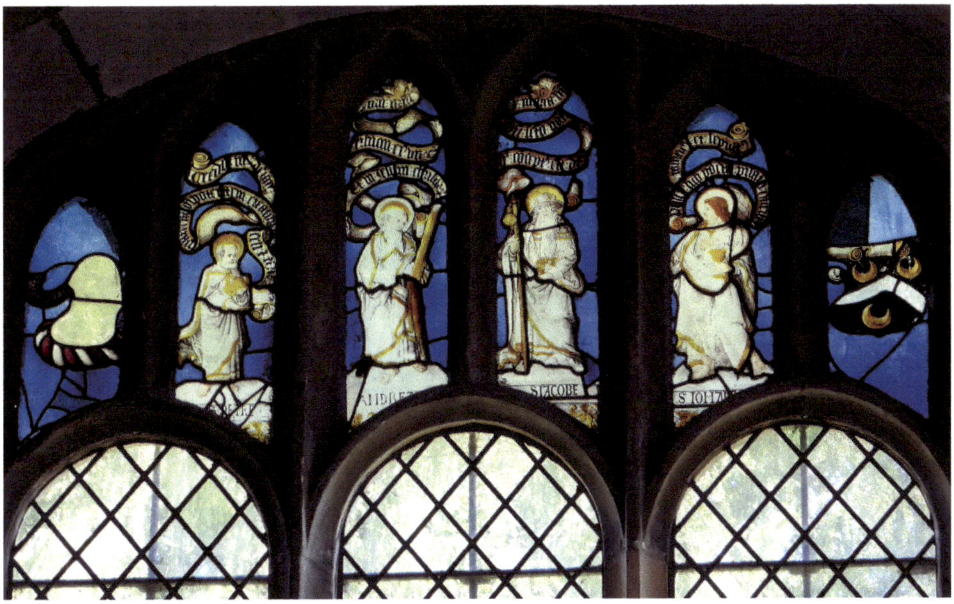

A few of the surviving tracery-lights in the chancel chapel windows depicting a series of Apostles in Renaissance style by Flemish glaziers, *c.* 1530.

in the chancel and chapels beyond. The most rewarding tombs flank the sanctuary, that on the north side bearing fine Tudor brasses to Sir George Throckmorton (d. 1553) and his wife Katherine with their many children below. Opposite is the grandest monument here, an imposing tomb in alabaster with effigies of Sir John Throckmorton (d. 1580) and his wife Marjorie lying beneath a huge canopy borne on fluted columns as if it were a six-poster bed. The carving is not of the highest quality, but the monument makes a bold statement.

Perhaps the most enjoyable features here are the fragments of late medieval/ early Renaissance stained glass in the traceries of the chancel windows: fine quality and obviously the work of Flemish glaziers, they provide tantalising glimpses of what we've lost (the original subjects are recorded as stipulated in Sir Robert's will). The side windows have tiny Apostles and saints against a blue background, while the east window has more substantial heraldic display and three sibyls in lavish costume (their heads Victorian replacements). There are earlier fragments in some nave windows and by contrast little Victorian glass. Substantial elements of late medieval woodwork also remain in the chancel, fairly plain and easily missed, but the four figure carvings are worth seeking out.

19. Coventry, Cathedral

Doing St Michael's Cathedral justice is of course a subject beyond the scope of this book as it is worthy of a one in its own right, thus an introduction will have to suffice here, but it is simply too important to be omitted, formerly one of the largest parish churches in the country, and latterly one of the most groundbreaking cathedrals that became a milestone of ecclesiastical art and design.

Coventry's Cathedral is a unique synthesis of old and new, born of wartime suffering and forged in the spirit of post-war optimism, famous for both its tortured history and being the most radically modern of Anglican cathedrals. Two cathedrals stand side by side: the ruins of the medieval building, destroyed by incendiary bombs in 1940, and the bold new building designed by Basil Spence and was opened in 1962.

It is a common misconception that Coventry lost its first cathedral in the wartime Blitz, but the bombs actually destroyed its second; the original medieval cathedral was the monastic St Mary's, a large cruciform building believed to have been similar in appearance to Lichfield Cathedral (whose diocese it shared). Tragically, it became the only English cathedral to be lost to the Reformation, after which it was quickly quarried away leaving only scant fragments, but enough evidence survives to indicate its rich decoration (some pieces were displayed nearby in the Priory Visitors Centre). Foundations of its apse were found during the building of the new cathedral in the 1950s; thus, technically, three cathedrals share the same site.

The mainly fifteenth-century St Michael's Church became the seat of the new diocese of Coventry in 1918 and, being one of the largest parish churches in the country, it was upgraded to cathedral status without structural changes (unlike most 'parish church' cathedrals created in the early twentieth century). It lasted in this role a mere twenty-two years before being burned to the ground in the 1940 Coventry Blitz, leaving only the outer walls and the magnificent tapering tower and spire (the extensive arcades and clerestories collapsed completely in the fire, precipitated by the roof reinforcement girders, installed in the Victorian restoration, which buckled in the intense heat).

The determination to rebuild the cathedral in some form was born on the day of the bombing; however, it wasn't until the mid-1950s that a competition was held and Sir Basil Spence's design was chosen. Spence had been so moved by experiencing the ruined church he resolved to retain it entirely to serve as a forecourt to the new church. He envisaged the two being linked by a glass screen wall so that the old church would be visible from within the new.

Built in 1957–62 and at a right-angle to the ruins, the new cathedral attracted controversy for its modern form, yet some modernists argued that it didn't go far enough. After all, there are echoes of the Gothic style in the great stone-mullioned windows of the nave and the net vaulting within (actually a free-standing canopy independent of the shell of the building). What is exceptional is the way art has been used as such an integral part of the building – a watershed moment, revolutionising the concept of religious art in Britain.

Spence employed some of the biggest names in contemporary art to contribute their vision to his. The exterior is adorned with Jacob Epstein's triumphant bronze figures of Archangel Michael (patron of the cathedral) vanquishing the Devil. At the entrance is the remarkable glass wall, engraved by John Hutton with strikingly stylised figures of saints and angels, and allowing the interior of the new to communicate with the ruin. Inside, the great tapestry of Christ in majesty surrounded by the evangelistic creatures draws the eye beyond the high altar; it was designed by Graham Sutherland and was the largest tapestry ever made.

However, one of the greatest features of Coventry is its wealth of modern stained glass, something Spence resolved to include having witnessed the

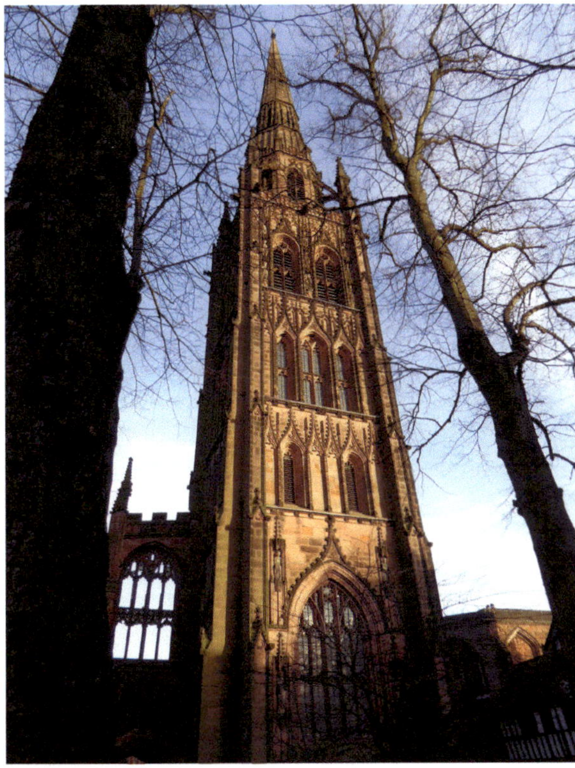

Right: The magnificent steeple of the former St Michael's Church, the third tallest medieval spire in the country (after Salisbury and Norwich cathedrals).

Below: The nave of Basil Spence's new cathedral, showing the synthesis of stark modernity and a surprisingly Gothic-inspired vault canopy.

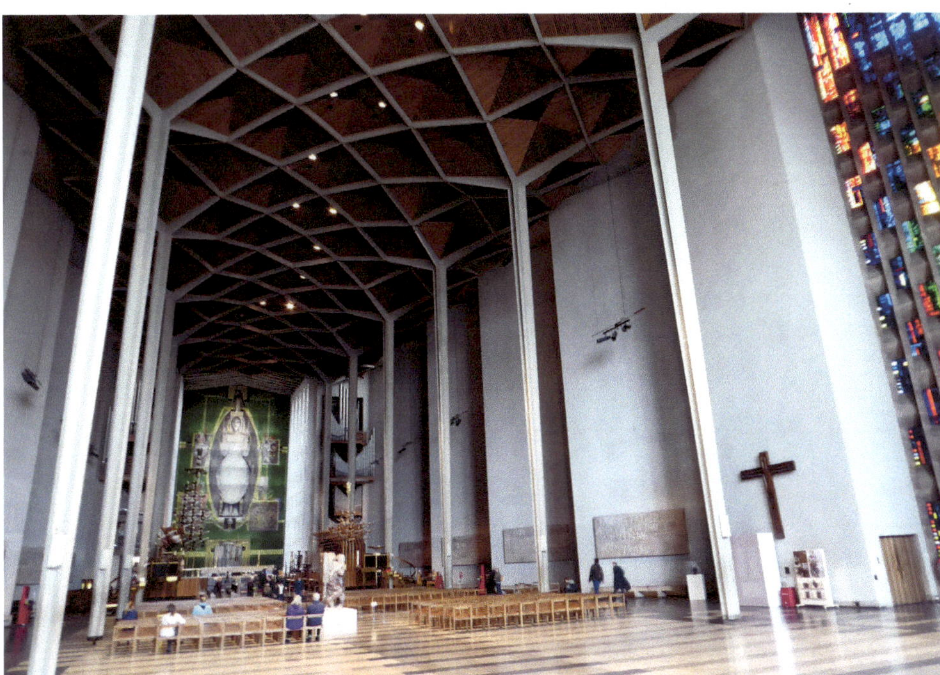

bleakness of Chartres Cathedral in wartime, when all its stained glass had been removed. The first window encountered upon entering is the enormous 'chess-board' baptistery window filled with stunning abstract glass by John Piper and Patrick Reyntiens, a symphony of glowing colour. The staggered nave walls are illuminated by ten narrow floor-to-ceiling windows filled with semi-abstract symbolic designs arranged in pairs of dominant colours (green, red, multi-coloured, purple/blue and gold) representing the soul's journey to maturity, and revealed gradually as one approaches the altar. This amazing project was the work of three designers lead by master glass artist Lawrence Lee of the Royal College of Art along with Keith New and Geoffrey Clarke (each artist designed three of the windows individually and all collaborated on the last).

The cathedral still dazzles the visitor with the boldness of its vision, but it was not a vision to be repeated, and few churches and cathedrals built since can claim to have embraced the synthesis of art and architecture in the inspiring way Basil Spence did at Coventry.

20. Coventry, Holy Trinity

Holy Trinity would have been the star attraction anywhere else, a majestic cruciform fifteenth-century Perpendicular church with a tapering central tower and spire, the second of Coventry's famous 'Three Spires'. However, it has always

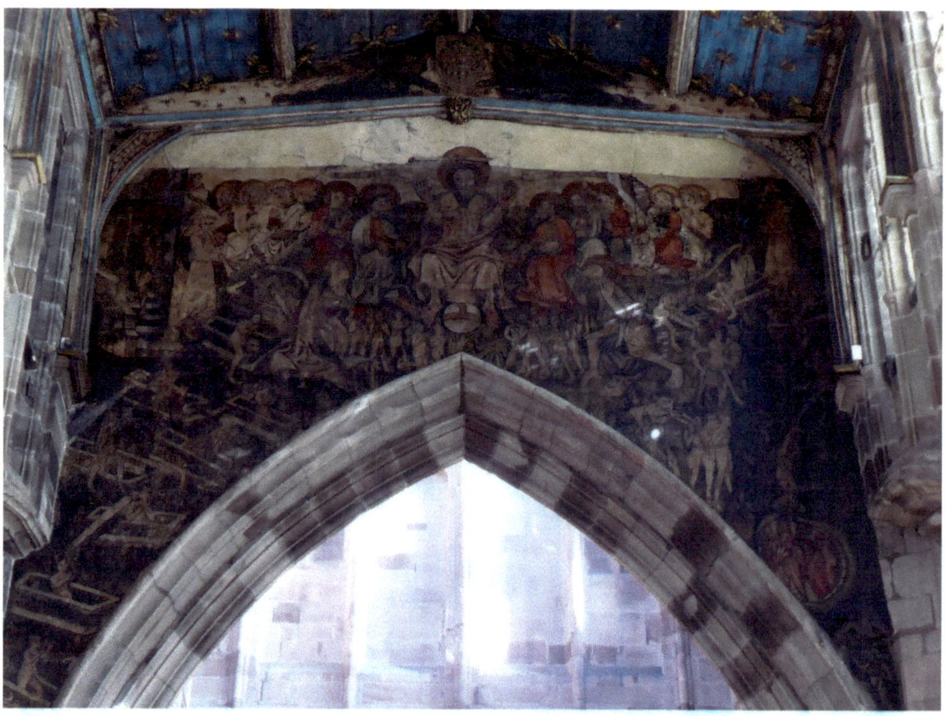

Holy Trinity Church, Coventry. The fifteenth-century Last Judgement or 'Doom' painting over the chancel arch, uncovered again in 2004 after being hidden for over a century beneath darkened varnish.

been overshadowed by larger neighbours, having been encircled by no less than three separate cathedrals throughout its history, a unique distinction! Holy Trinity was founded by the monks of the adjoining priory to act as a parish church for its lay tenants, thus it is ironic that it has long outlived the parent building.

The earliest part is the north porch, which dates from the thirteenth century, but the majority of the building represents a more ambitious phase in fifteenth-century Perpendicular style, resulting in the present cruciform arrangement with small transepts and extra chapels on the north side and consequently the church's broadly rectangular footprint. These chapels were some of many in the church that served the city's separate guilds in medieval times.

The church has experienced much restoration, most notably the rebuilding of its spire after it was blown down in a storm in 1665. The east end of the chancel was extended in 1786 (in sympathetic style) and much of the exterior was refaced in the early nineteenth century in then fashionable Bath stone (which clashes with the original red sandstone).

The church luckily escaped major damage during the Coventry Blitz in 1940, largely thanks to the vigilance of firewatchers who spent a perilous night on the roof tackling incendiaries. The main loss was the Victorian stained glass in the east and west windows, which were replaced with much more fetching glass in the post-war restoration.

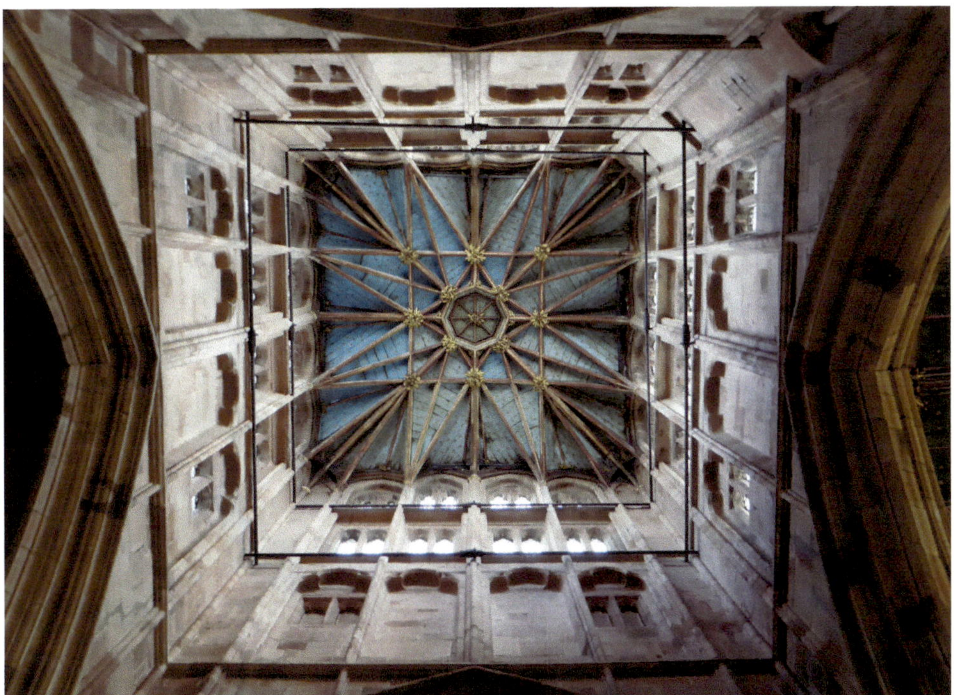

The view into Holy Trinity's central tower with its beautiful star-vaulted ceiling inserted by G. G. Scott in 1854 when he removed the belfry and ringing chamber to restore this space to view from below.

The most recent restoration involved uncovering the fifteenth-century Doom painting over the chancel arch in 2004. Hidden under blackened varnish since it's rediscovery in the early Victorian period, it has now been revealed to be one of the most complete and important medieval Last Judgement murals in the country. There is further painting contemporary with this on the exquisite nave ceiling, painted a beautiful dusty blue with large kneeling angels flanking coats of arms on every rafter.

There are only a handful of monuments and most of the furnishings date from G. G. Scott's 1850s restoration (as does the magnificent vaulted ceiling, high above the crossing) but there are some notable medieval survivals in the rare stone pulpit and the brass eagle lectern, both fifteenth century, along with a fine set of carved misericords originating from the former Whitefriars monastery church. Just a few fragments of medieval glass survive in the north-west chapel.

21. Coventry, St John the Baptist

St John's sits at the entrance to Spon Street, that rare enclave of medieval architecture in Coventry's mostly post-war city centre. Being on the fringe of the city's heart it generally gets less attention from visitors, thus one feels that in any other setting it would be far more celebrated; indeed, George Gilbert Scott, who restored the church in 1877, considered it 'one of the most beautiful churches in

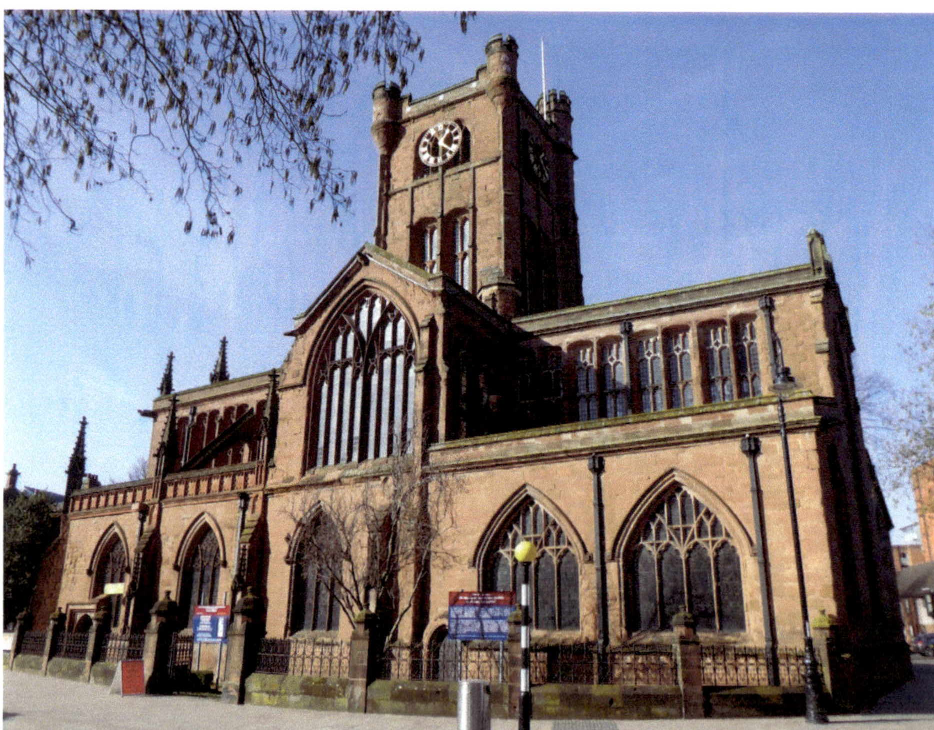

St John the Baptist's Church, Coventry. A fine example of a fifteenth-century Perpendicular church, a landmark holding out against a much-changed urban environment.

England'. The church luckily escaped major damage in the November 1940 Blitz that destroyed so much else in the city, beyond the loss of much (but not all) of its Victorian stained glass.

St John's was founded in 1342 by Queen Isabella, mother of Edward III, but most of what we see today is fifteenth-century work, though evidently of different phases. The church sits on a relatively small site, but what it lacks in length and width it gains in height, and with its tapering and unusually narrow clerestory windows and central tower it gives the impression of a cathedral in miniature. The tower has oddly corbelled-out turrets at its corners, an over-exaggeration of the original design by Scott; his main intervention on the exterior otherwise was the renewal of much of the stonework, since warm red sandstone is one of the least resistant to weathering.

The interior is surprisingly light for a sandstone church, the result of the large Perpendicular windows and extensive clerestory that creates a 'glass cage' effect in the higher parts of the church. It is also rather narrow, which further accentuates the sense of height, a good example of architectural limitations and constraints turned to an advantage. There are some good medieval carvings surviving higher up. The tower was designed with an internal 'lantern' stage to be viewed from below and retains its original star-vault halfway up, but alas this is currently hidden from view.

The lack of historic furnishings or monuments is explained by the history of the church, since it actually ceased to be used for worship in the 1590s and for

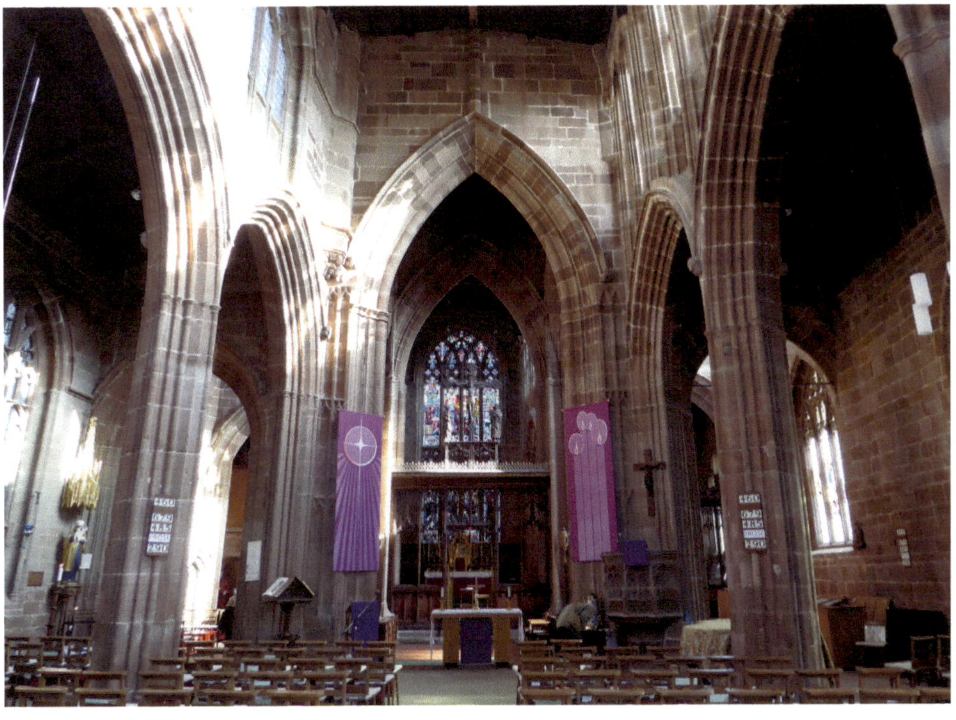

The warm red-sandstone interior, rectangular in plan but cruciform in form and volume.

several centuries suffered various indignities of secular use, most infamously as a prison for Scottish rebels captured after the Battle of Preston during the Civil War in 1648 (these rebels, loyal to the king, were shunned in the Parliamentarian-held city, thus the phrase being 'sent to Coventry' was born). Other uses included as stables, a market and a winding and dying house for cloth, before being eventually restored to church use in the nineteenth century. We should be glad that being put to other uses at least preserved the structure through its centuries of hibernation.

The church possesses an interesting mixture of stained glass, from Victorian and Edwardian pieces that survived the bombing, to the more prominent and colourful windows installed in the 1950s, most noticeably the rich east window by Margaret Aldrich Rope. However, it is interesting to note how the post-war glass here predates the nearby Cathedral's windows by only a few years, but is still highly figurative and traditional in approach, thus still a far cry from the revolutionary new works that Coventry became famous for less than a decade later.

22. Curdworth, St Nicholas

Curdworth's fine red-sandstone church consists of a largely Norman nave and chancel (most windows were later enlarged during the medieval period) to which was added a handsome Perpendicular tower in *c.* 1460. Its interior has a tunnel-like effect owing to the lack of aisles and low Norman chancel arch (with chevron decoration) which permits only a glimpse of the chancel beyond, though relieved by later window-like openings or squints on each side. Above the arch sits an organ gallery whose ornate neo-Gothic woodwork dominates the view eastwards.

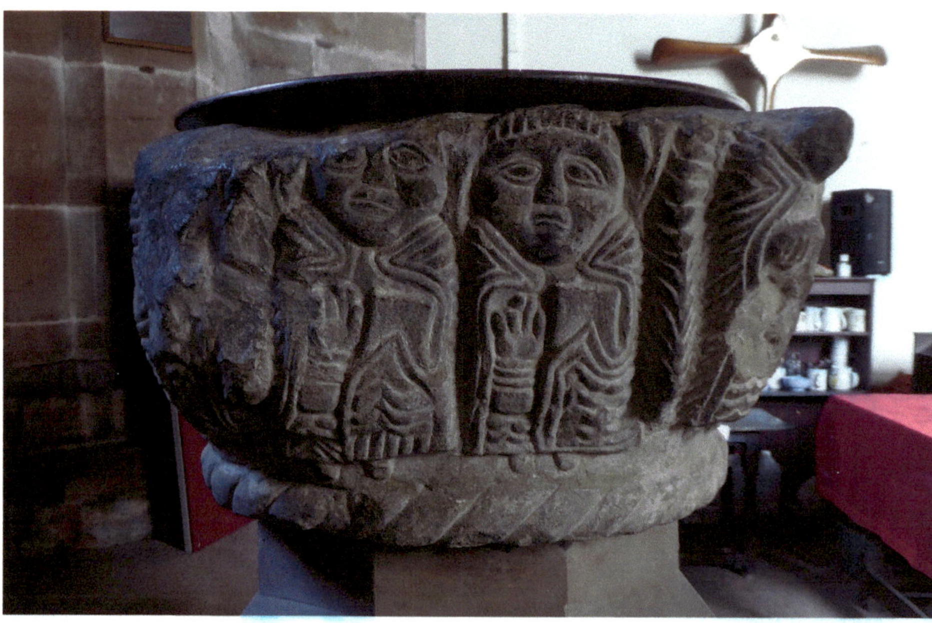

St Nicholas' Church, Curdworth. The richly carved font with its squat figures, generally considered to be early twelfth-century Norman work (or possibly late Anglo-Saxon).

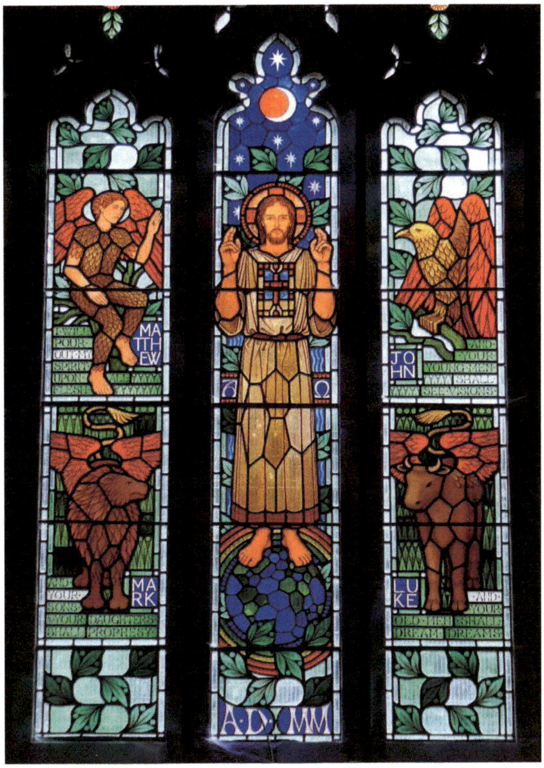

The Millennium Window at St Nicholas' by Meg Lawrence, 2001, depicting Christ surrounded by the emblems of the Four Evangelists.

The most outstanding twelfth-century Romanesque survival, however, is the carved font at the west end of the nave, adorned with very squat figures and beasts in a primitive style. It was found buried under the floor in 1895 and though its upper edges are damaged it is a remarkable piece of provincial Norman work.

Much more of antiquarian interest survives here including substantial remains of medieval wall painting in the splays of the remaining Norman windows and a tiny but fine fragment of a reredos with a damaged re-coloured relief presumed to be Archangel Gabriel. The thirteenth-century parish chest behind the altar astonishingly almost extends the full width of the church, while nearby are a few fourteenth-century tiles adorned with the head of a king and a rare depiction of the alphabet.

Refreshingly there is no Victorian glass in the church but a fine 1912 east window by Geoffrey Webb, complemented by a rich millennium window on the south side of the nave from 2001 designed in traditional style by Meg Lawrence.

23. Great Packington, St James

The estate church of Great Packington is one of the most important and uniquely designed classical churches in Britain, built in 1789–90 to the design of Joseph Bonomi. Standing in splendid solitude, the red-brick exterior appears as a square, somewhat domestic-looking block, topped eccentrically by four stone corner towers crowned with cupolas, giving this church a unique silhouette.

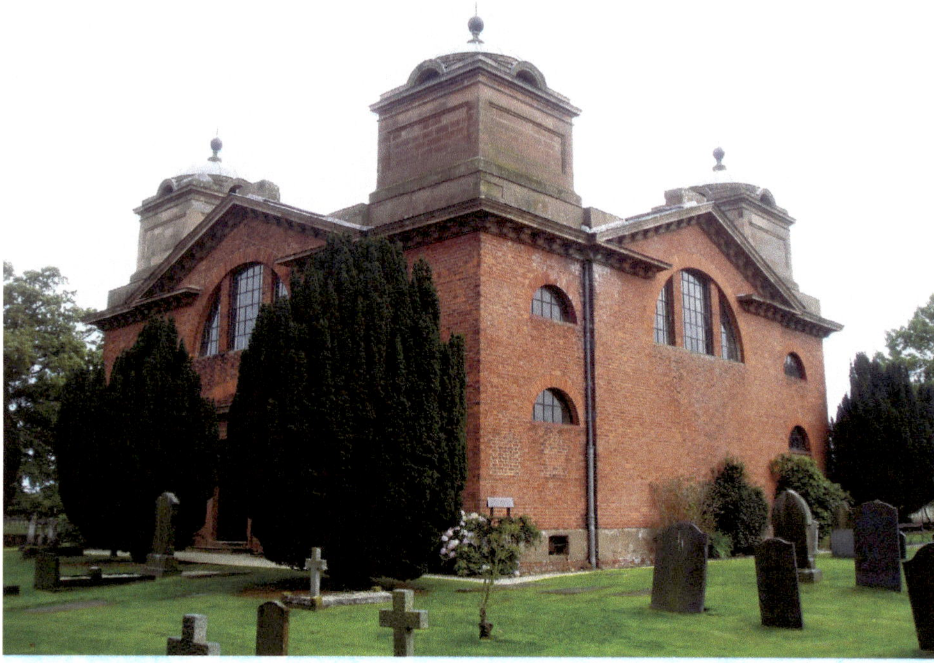

St James' Church, Great Packington. The remarkable estate church designed by Joseph Bonomi in 1789, a Roman-inspired brick square with cupola-crowned corner towers.

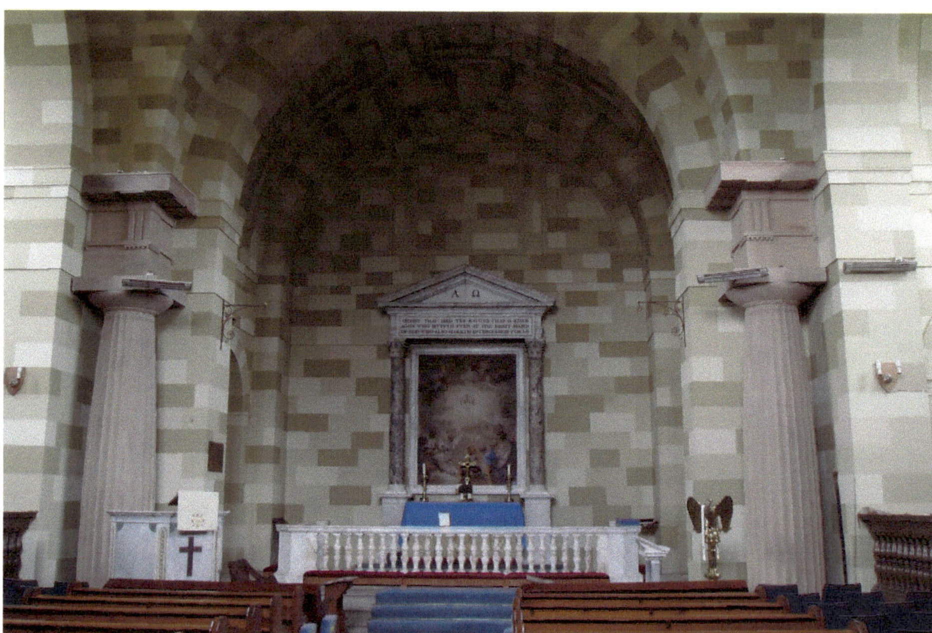

Interior of the 1789 church, illustrating how the square building is subdivided at the corners within to create a cruciform interior.

The semi-circular lunette windows are directly inspired by the architecture of ancient Rome (the architect's native city).

The interior is a remarkable contrast, finished throughout with plaster but painted to resemble masonry (recently restored) and in the form of an equal-ended Greek cross, with the corner spaces beneath the towers separated by heavy arches and sturdy Doric columns. It is a space of intriguing austerity, relieved only by a pedimented altarpiece framing a painting by Jean Francois Rigaud depicting a shining IHS monogram amid angels and clouds.

Of the previous medieval church here only one relic remains, a pair of recumbent Elizabethan effigies in painted wood and plaster from a once much larger monument to members of the Fisher family.

24. Grendon, All Saints

Grendon is one of north Warwickshire's most rewarding churches, though somewhat remote and thus relatively little known. The medieval building has been much altered and restored, the dignified west tower dating only from 1845 (stylistically pre-Victorian) while the whitewashed interior with its plastered ceilings and copious woodwork impart a late Georgian character. The real interest here is in the fascinating collection of furnishings and memorials to members of the Chetwynd family.

This church is an 'Aladdin's cave' of interesting things and the post-Reformation woodwork in particular is a real delight, most notably the enclosed

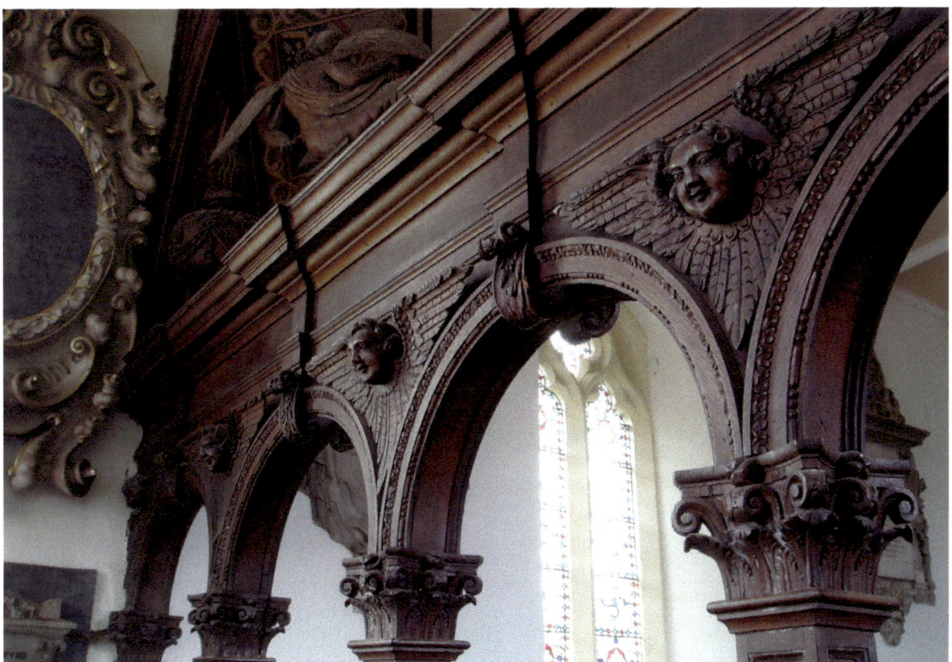

Detail of the exuberantly carved south aisle screen at All Saints' Church, Grendon, an example of the lavish post-Reformation woodwork that makes this church so special.

churchwarden's pew beneath the organ gallery at the west end, dating from 1618 and originally from St Mary's, Stafford. It is adorned with Jacobean ornamentation but intriguingly includes an apparently mid-sixteenth century low-relief panel depicting Hermes on its northern face. The other showpiece among the furnishings is the splendid screen of *c.* 1680 in the south aisle that encloses the private Chetwynd pew, with arched openings with winged cherubs' heads carved in the spandrels and two complete angels perched above. Mention must also be made of the fine altar rails and surprisingly Catholic-looking *c.* 1740 reredos carving of Christ in the chancel.

There are memorials aplenty, the earliest being an alabaster effigy of an unknown fifteenth-century lady and an incised slab to Margaret Chetwynd (d. 1539). The rest mainly take the form of tablets aside from the life-size grieving woman by an urn commemorating Mary Chetwynd (d. 1750). The church has an unusually extensive display of heraldic hatchments, perhaps the largest collection in the county.

25. Hampton Lucy, St Peter ad Vincula

Hampton Lucy (close to Charlecote Park) boasts one of the most outstanding churches of the pre-Victorian Gothic Revival, dating from 1822 to 1826 and built to the design of Thomas Rickman. It is a magnificent building of golden-hued stone, comprising a spacious aisled nave with plaster-vaulted ceilings and a soaring west

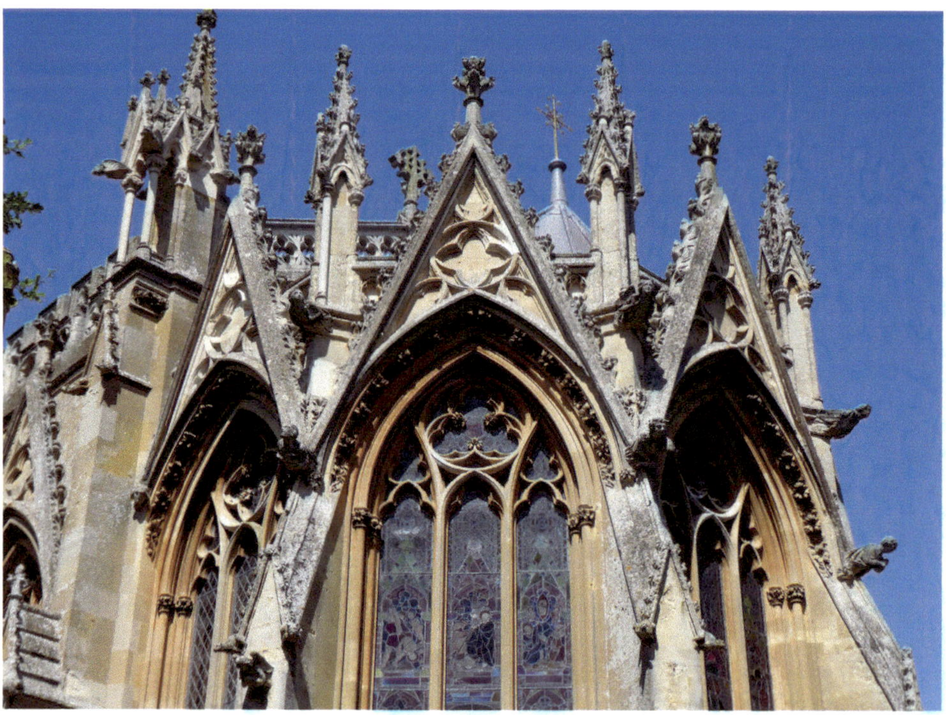

St Peter ad Vincula, Hampton Lucy. Detail of the florid Victorian Gothic polygonal apse added by George Gilbert Scott in 1856 to Thomas Rickman's more restrained 1820s Gothic Revival church.

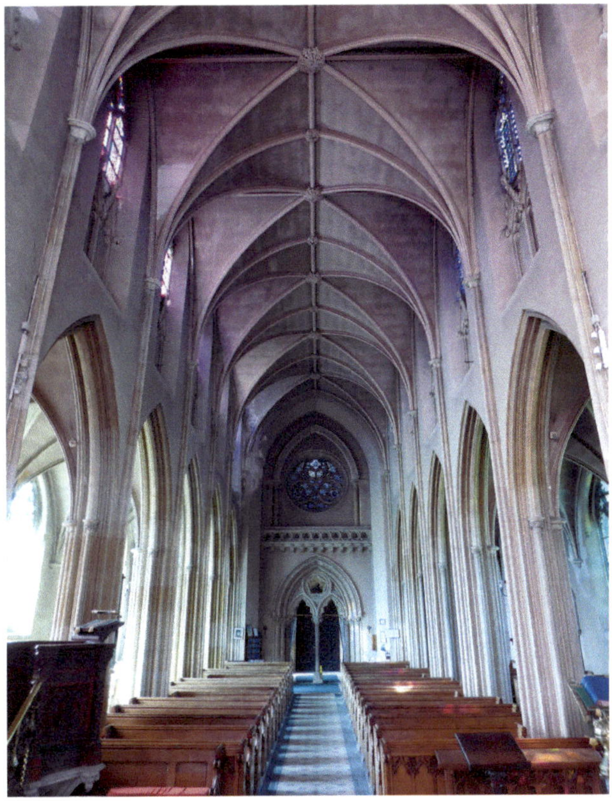

Interior of the nave looking westwards, a serene essay in 1820s Gothic Revival by Thomas Rickman.

tower. The chancel was altered in 1856 when George Gilbert Scott added the elaborate polygonal apse in ornate full-blown Victorian Gothic, a masterpiece in its own right.

The interior is thrillingly cathedral-like, the eye drawn to the glowing apse through a nave subdued by coloured light from its richly patterned clerestory windows, casting their varied hues across the vaulting on sunny days. The most notable glass is from 1837 by Thomas Willement in the three apse windows, formerly contained in one huge window before Rickman's east end was altered. The Gilbert Scott apse is the visual climax of the interior, inspired by French Gothic and elaborately vaulted.

This is a church to savour for its architectural beauty, rather than contents or history; what it lacks in these departments it easily makes up for in sheer spectacle.

26. Hillmorton, St John the Baptist

A fine old church well worth exploring but less well known, St John the Baptist's serves what is now a large suburb of Rugby and yet retains a country church atmosphere, being cut off from the town by the railway (and thus approached bizarrely through a tunnel under the railway line). It's a mainly thirteenth-/fourteenth-century building, the west tower is of a rich red sandstone while the body of the building has been patched up at various dates, giving it an attractively un-restored aged patina.

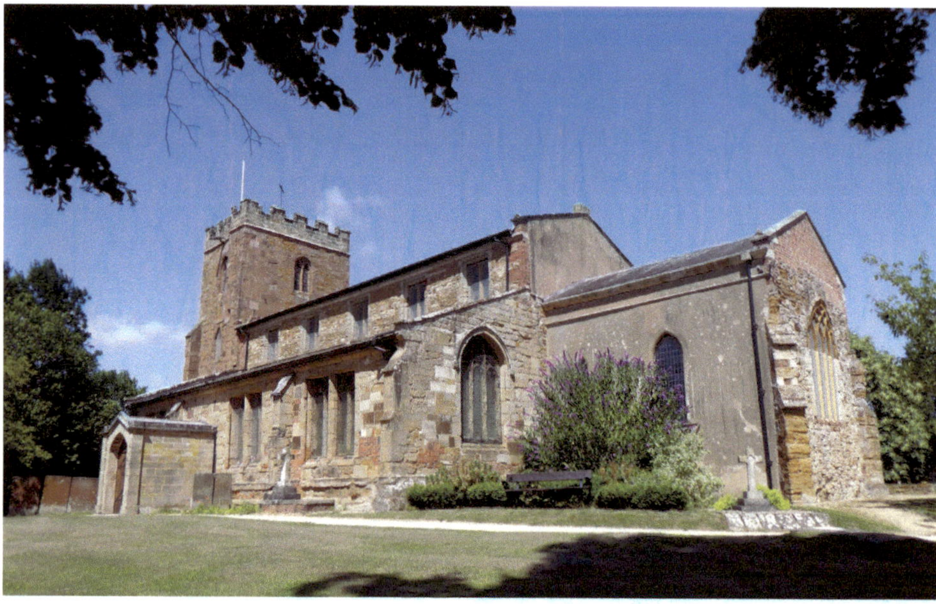

The richly toned and textured ancient church of St John the Baptist, Hillmorton, separated from the suburbs by railway and canal.

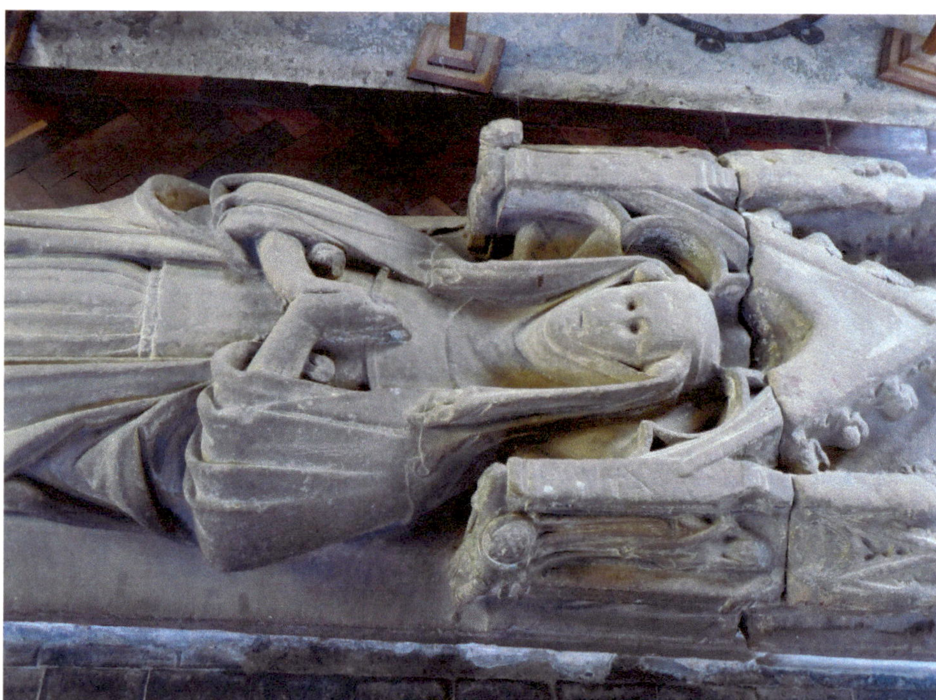

The early fourteenth-century wimpled lady in the south aisle, believed to be Margaret de Astley. The canopy around her head contains small figures and traces of colouring.

The interior is equally largely unspoilt, retaining a post-Reformation feel with its furnishings, royal arms and whitewashed walls (strangely only the chancel and south aisle have been scraped back to the stonework). Victorian glass is confined to two south aisle windows (including one strange piecemeal affair) and a single light in the chancel; the main east window with its intersecting tracery is left plain.

The main items of interest here are the monuments: three medieval tombs and an elegant brass of an early fifteenth-century lady. Of the effigies, by far the best is the early fourteenth-century wimpled lady in the south aisle believed to be Margaret de Astley with a large canopy over her head, within which are small figures and traces of colour. The nearby knight is more damaged while the thirteenth-century priest under an arch in the north aisle (almost hidden behind benches) is also badly mutilated.

27. Honiley, St John the Baptist

A modestly sized but exceptional baroque church consisting of a short nave and apsed chancel, terminated at the west end by a very individually designed tower and spire. The building was constructed in 1723 and was reputedly based on a sketch made by Sir Christopher Wren while dining with a friend at neighbouring

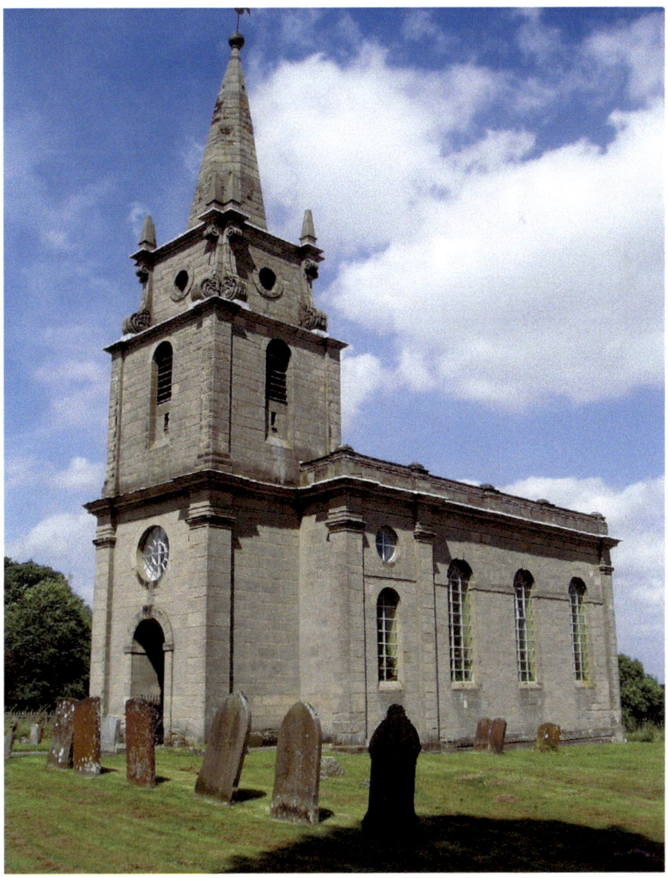

The handsome baroque St John the Baptist Church, Honiley, of 1723. Its architect is unknown but there is a legend that Christopher Wren supplied a sketch in his final years.

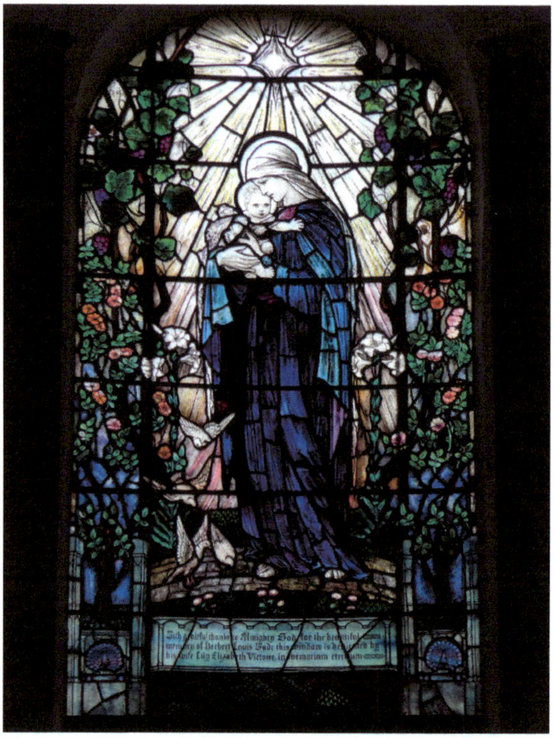

The Arts and Crafts glass in the east window by Theodora Salusbury, one of three beautiful windows she created for the apse here at Honiley in 1924–26.

Honiley Hall (Wren had recently purchased nearby Wroxall Abbey estate, lending credence to the story). Whoever the architect was, it is certainly a building of some quality and distinction.

Within all is neat, whitewashed simplicity, with the original box pews and organ gallery at the west end. The plain decor is relieved in the apse, adorned by pilasters with Corinthian capitals that finish strangely short of the ceiling. This would be an intact eighteenth-century interior if not for the windows, with textured panes replacing the original leaded plain glazing of the nave and stained glass introduced into the apse.

The three apse windows are superb Arts and Crafts pieces by Theodora Salusbury from 1924 to 1926, adding great richness and providing a fitting climax to the interior (churches of this period were designed for clear glass, yet here the ensemble works beautifully to create a focus, as do the Burne-Jones windows at Birmingham Cathedral). The artist's signature is most distinctive, as she simply used the image of a peacock which can be found at the bottom of all three windows.

28. Honington, All Saints

One of the most memorable churches in south Warwickshire, this was rebuilt in 1684, leaving the fourteenth-century ironstone tower of the previous church attached to a limestone body in the style of Wren. It sits in a picturesque churchyard next to the private grounds of Honington Hall, somewhat engulfed by trees to its north and west.

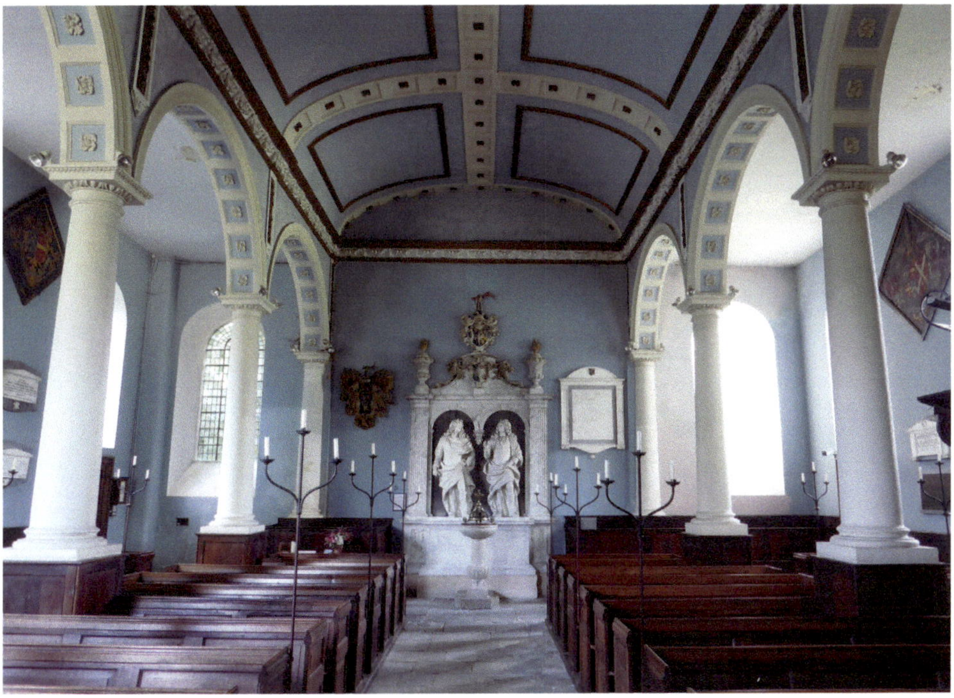

The nave of the baroque All Saints' Church at Honington of 1684, looking westwards towards the imposing Parker Monument.

Within is a gem of a baroque interior, mostly coloured pale blue with white and gilded accents, replete with most of its original late seventeenth-century furnishings (the box pews reduced in height by the Victorians, who also introduced the incongruous Hardman glass in four windows). It is an opulent space, crowned by a curved ceiling and richly carved royal arms above the apse.

The real treasures here are the baroque monuments, the finest dominating the west end of the nave with elegantly swaggering statues of Sir Henry Parker and his son Hugh (d. 1713 and 1712 respectively). Another in the south aisle features a seated putto with a grotesquely exaggerated cranium, often described as one of the ugliest of cherubs or a 'nightmare of a sculpture'!

29. Ilmington, St Mary

Set in the hills of south-west Warwickshire, this delightful church of honey-coloured stone is somewhat elusive but well worth seeking out. It occupies the far end of a lush narrow churchyard, framed by foliage and memorably approached via a tree-lined footpath.

The building is essentially Norman with later additions. Much of the twelfth-century church remains (without aisles), particularly the lower half of the tower, the nave with Norman doorways (both with later alterations that is now glazed on the north side) and in the long, cavernous interior the low chancel arch has carved capitals on one side (the tower arch is plainer but far more impressive).

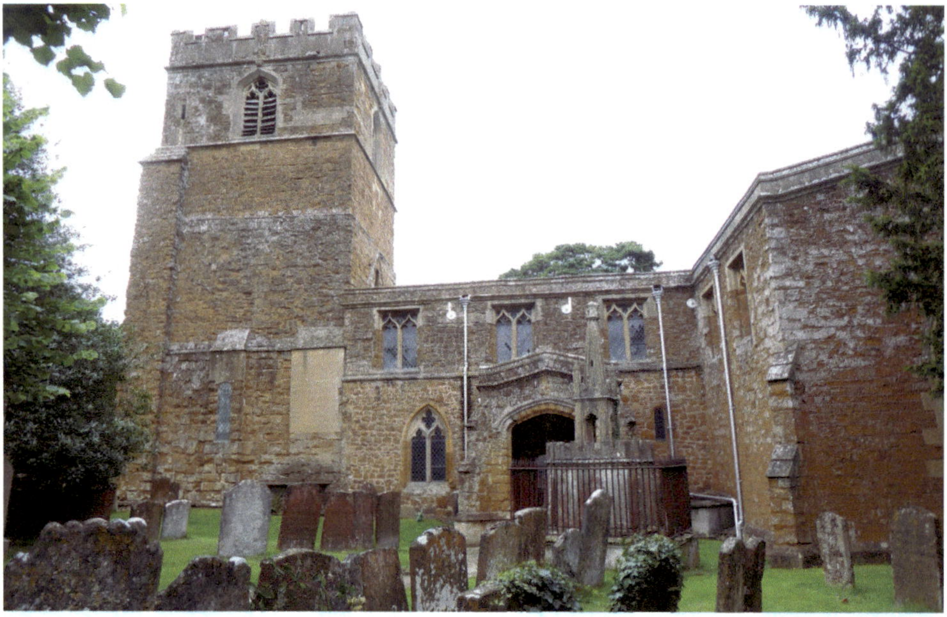

The picturesque, ancient St Mary's Church at Ilmington evolved greatly over the centuries. Note the surviving Norman window east of the porch balanced by a fourteenth-century Decorated one to the west, and finally a row of fifteenth-century square-headed clerestory windows above with the wall raised to accommodate them.

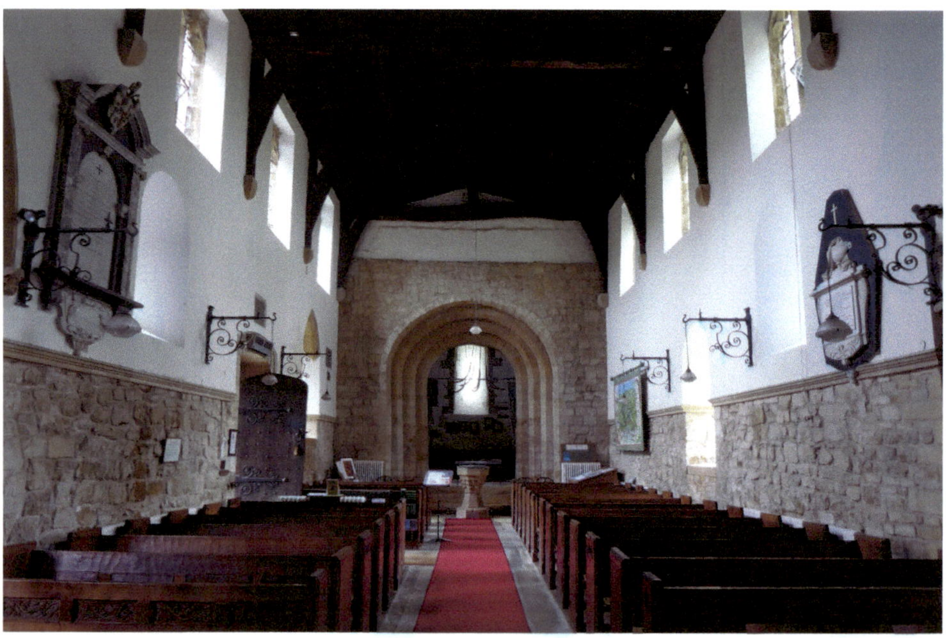

View looking westwards in the nave towards the tower arch, for some strange reason a far more impressive opening than the chancel arch (where worship was actually focussed) to the east.

The chancel dates from the following century and features curious arched recesses around its walls within. The spacious north transept appears to be of similar date but much altered and, like the nave, was raised in the fifteenth century to include a clerestory. Finally, the carefully copied south transept was added in 1846 to give the cruciform church we see today.

This is a church to be enjoyed more for its architecture and antiquity than its contents, but it does hold some features of note, such as the damaged effigy of a priest and an oddly designed font at the west end. Outside, near the south porch, is a quirky eighteenth-century Gothic memorial in the form of a plinth crowned by a small steeple.

30. Knowle, St John the Baptist, St Lawrence and St Anne

This stately building is a good example of a Perpendicular Midland church, mostly of fifteenth-century date and profusely adorned on the south side with battlements, pinnacles and gargoyles. Two different local sandstones were used – white for the earlier parts, red for the later – adding to the appeal of the exterior. Most of the church was likely completed by 1416 when a chantry college was founded here.

The interior is spacious, with the nave flanked by aisles and the chancel extending beyond a superb late medieval wooden screen. There are medieval stalls with ten misericords (mostly foliate designs, except two with animals) and sedilia

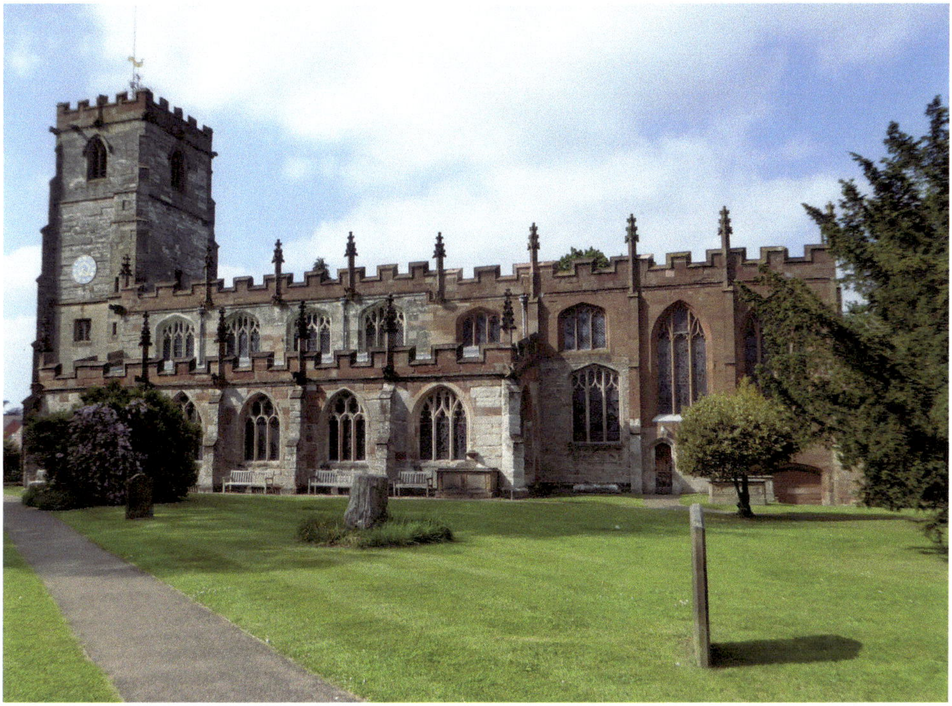

The handsome late medieval church at Knowle viewed from the south. The bulk of the building was completed in 1416 in grey stone, the reddish-sandstone elements being finished in a later phase.

niches far too high up for use as seating since the lowering of the floor (following removal of a passageway that once ran beneath the altar, its blocked entrances still visible externally).

There is an interesting mixture of stained glass from several Victorian and later studios, an extensive and varied collection including notable Arts and Crafts windows, one by Veronica Whall and another in rich purples and pinks by Theodora Salusbury. On the north side, separated by a stone screen, is a beautifully decorated chapel dedicated as a war memorial which also has fine glass.

31. Lapworth, St Mary

Lapworth is one of the most handsome and unusually configured medieval parish churches in Warwickshire. The visitor generally approaches from the north where the sturdy tower and spire stand guard like a sentinel, unusual in standing apart from the main building and originally detached but now linked by a passageway to the north aisle, making the church almost as wide as it is long. The west end, too, is remarkably configured, with a projecting chapel or relic chamber set above an archway, allowing passage across the churchyard below.

The church dates mainly from the thirteenth to fifteenth centuries, with an impressive nave clerestory a prominent external feature, but within it is possible to discern traces of previous Norman windows embedded below. There is much

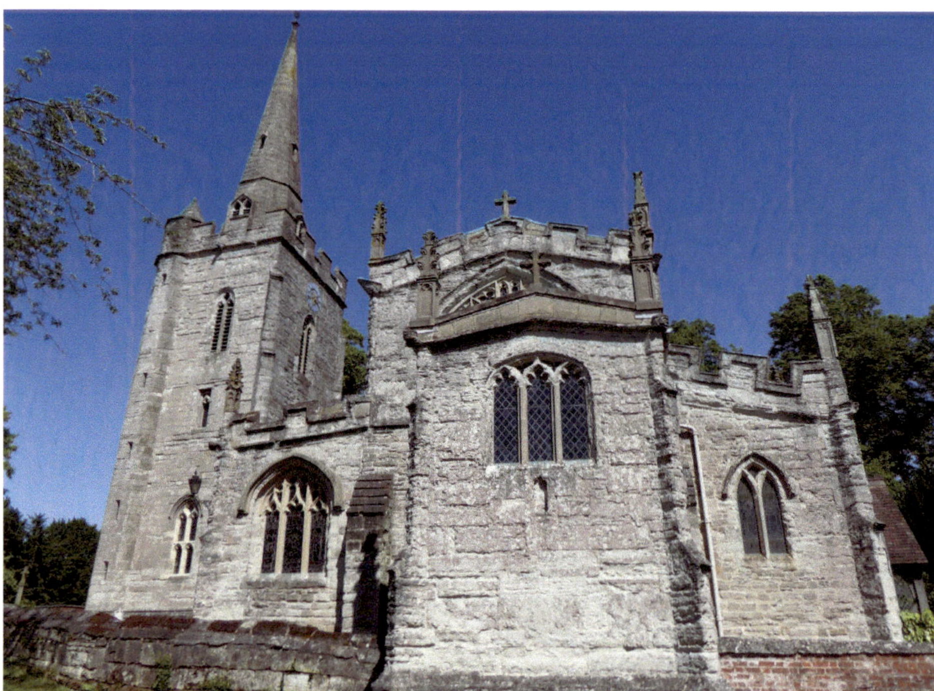

The unusual form of St Mary's Church, Lapworth, here viewed from the west, showing the off-centre projecting chapel over an archway (permitting a circuit of the church within the churchyard's boundaries) and the formerly detached tower and spire to the north.

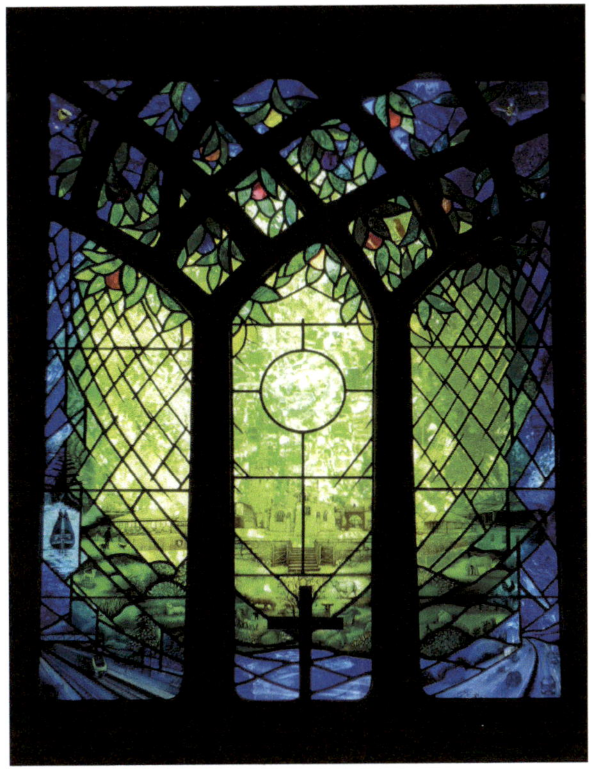

Newly inserted window in the north chapel of St Mary's, with stonework evoking the branches of a tree and glass designed and painted by Tony Naylor in 2015.

of interest in this pleasant interior, from quirky carvings high in the nave to the fourteenth-century font carved with head-corbels.

The 1860s stained glass by Clayton & Bell in the chancel is some of their best work, and the busy 1922 war memorial window by Richard Stubington is also excellent, if rather more sobering. The north chapel also recently benefitted from a newly inserted window in the formerly blank east wall with beautiful contemporary glass by Tony Naylor. The outstanding memorial is from 1928 commemorating Florence Bradshaw, bearing a lovely low relief Madonna and Child by Eric Gill.

32. Leamington Spa, All Saints

Leamington Spa's immense, cathedral-like parish church cannot fail to impress with its astonishing ambition. Construction began in 1843 over the site of a much more modest building, the bulk being completed in the following years by J. C. Jackson, though the west end of the nave and the soaring south-west tower weren't added until 1898–1902 by Sir Arthur Blomfield. A crossing tower with spire was originally intended, but only a stump was built owing to insufficient funds, though a smaller clock tower with steeple was added to the north transept, giving the church its distinctive outline.

The interior is impressively spacious and full of grandeur (if a touch gloomy). The west end was partitioned to form a gallery with parish rooms below in 1986

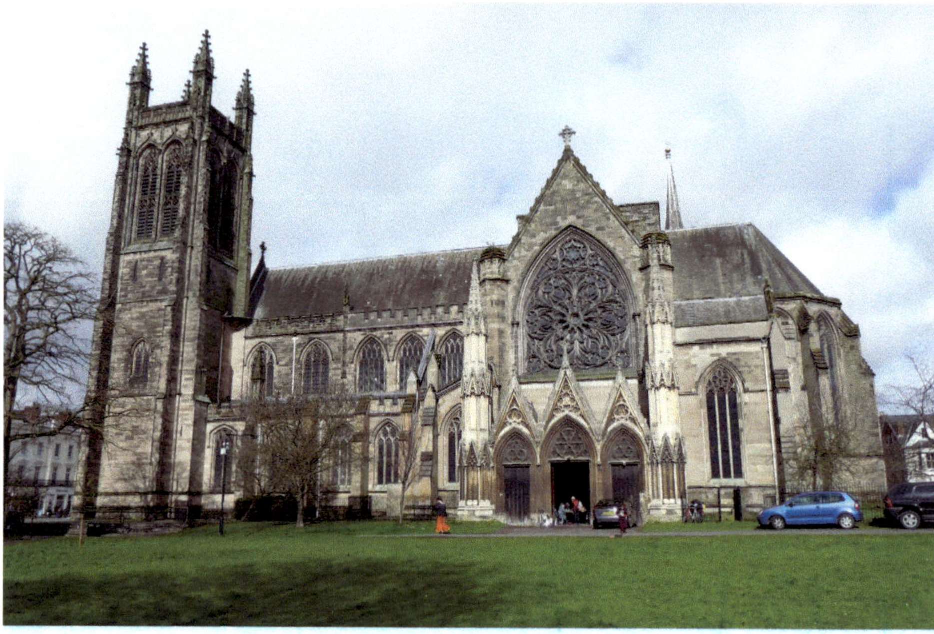

All Saints' Church, Leamington Spa, viewed from the south, with the junction visible halfway along the nave between the original construction of 1843 and Sir Arthur Blomfield's west end and south-west tower, added in 1898–1904.

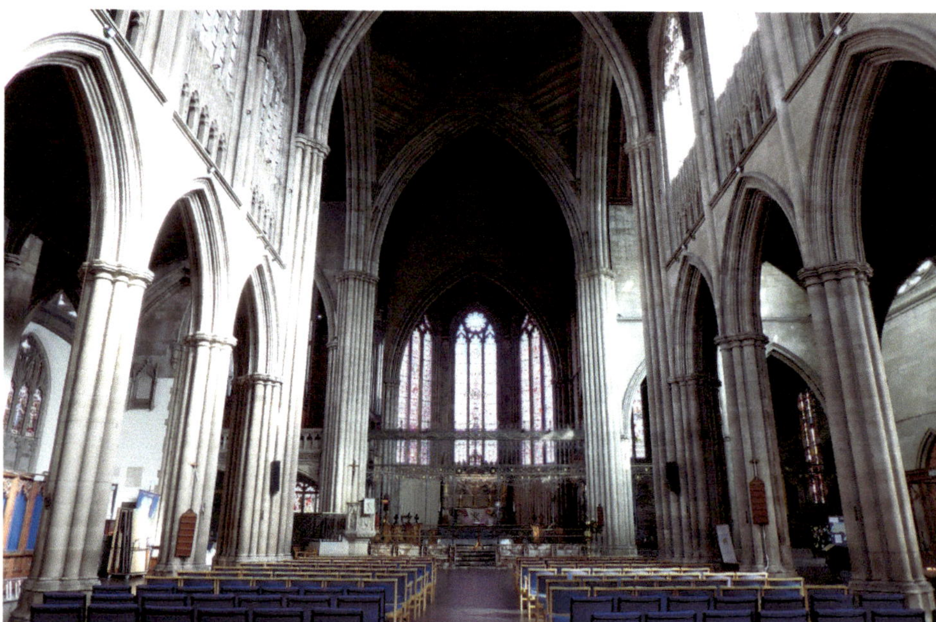

The cathedral-like interior of All Saints' Church looking towards the apse with its soaring windows by Chance Bros of Birmingham (in part shown at the Great Exhibition of 1851).

so one can no longer enjoy the full vista looking eastwards, but it is still quite the spectacle. The apse and transepts are largely French Gothic in style with enormous elaborately designed rose windows based on examples in Rouen (alas, lacking stained glass). The apse windows are among the tallest of their kind in any English parish church, containing rich glass by Chance Bros of Birmingham shown at the Great Exhibition of 1851 (and greatly improved by recent restoration). There is much glass of the Victorian period, though surprisingly little of it by the better-known studios (even the three Kempe-style windows are actually by his follower Herbert Bryans).

This is a church to be visited for its scale and vision as much as anything, a great explosion of Victorian Gothic in the heart of a Regency town, a dark, brooding presence on the townscape embodying architectural theatre at its most dramatic.

33. Leamington Spa, St Mark

Leamington Spa has an excellent collection of Victorian churches, and St Mark's in New Milverton is one of the most handsome buildings of its date. This vast, imposing edifice was built in 1879 by George Gilbert Scott Jr, one of his few surviving churches and best works. It displays a mixture of Decorated and Perpendicular forms in its huge traceried windows, all executed in an attractive blend of brick with stone dressings, an impressive addition to the landscape of the town and a major landmark in its own right.

It is light and spacious inside, though subdued by much Victorian glass – all Hardman in the nave along with some by Kempe in the chancel, while the huge east window is by lesser-known firm Cox & Buckley. The nave ceiling is plain and painted light blue, but the rest of the building has attractive rib vaulting

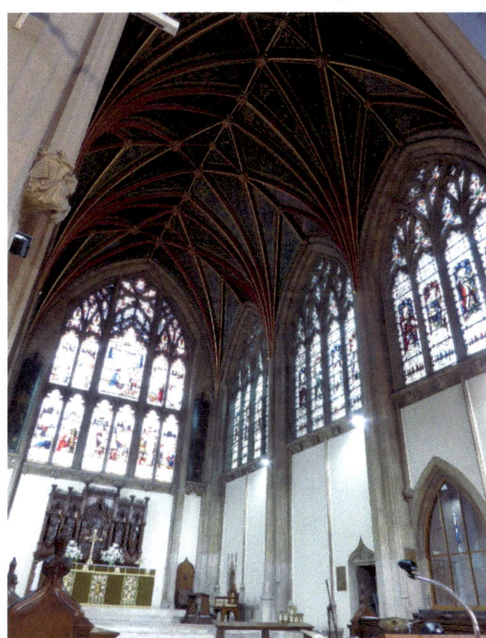

The impressive interior of the St Mark's chancel with its immense windows and colourful wooden ceiling vault.

throughout, reaching a climax in the chancel vault which is much busier with rich stencilling. The chancel windows are huge and, combined with the soaring height of this majestic space, evoke a cathedral or major college-chapel. The six-light east window here has quite peculiar tracery, with the central mullion absent from the upper register to enable a central Crucifixion group to feature (an odd arrangement I've not seen elsewhere).

The furnishings are contemporary with the church, the best being the rich organ case in the north transept (decorated again by Hardman) and the alabaster font with its dramatically tapering wooden cover.

34. Lillington, Our Lady

Our Lady's Roman Catholic church in Lillington (now a suburb of Leamington Spa) was opened in 1963 and is one of the most stunning modern churches in the Midlands. Designed by local architect Henry Fedeski, it is crowned by a slender copper spire and built on an ambitious scale, cruciform with each limb equal in length aside from the slightly longer nave. The outstanding element here is the sheer abundance of (mostly) abstract stained glass, bathing the interior in a magical kaleidoscopic light.

Entering the church is a moment to savour, the eyes drawn to the radiant colours on either side while the focal point is ironically the only unglazed wall in the church (post-war church architects generally seem to have a penchant for blank end walls), a large monogram in mosaic instead dominates the interior. The altar is centrally placed in the crossing, though may have been conceived originally for the chancel behind as this space now seems strangely empty.

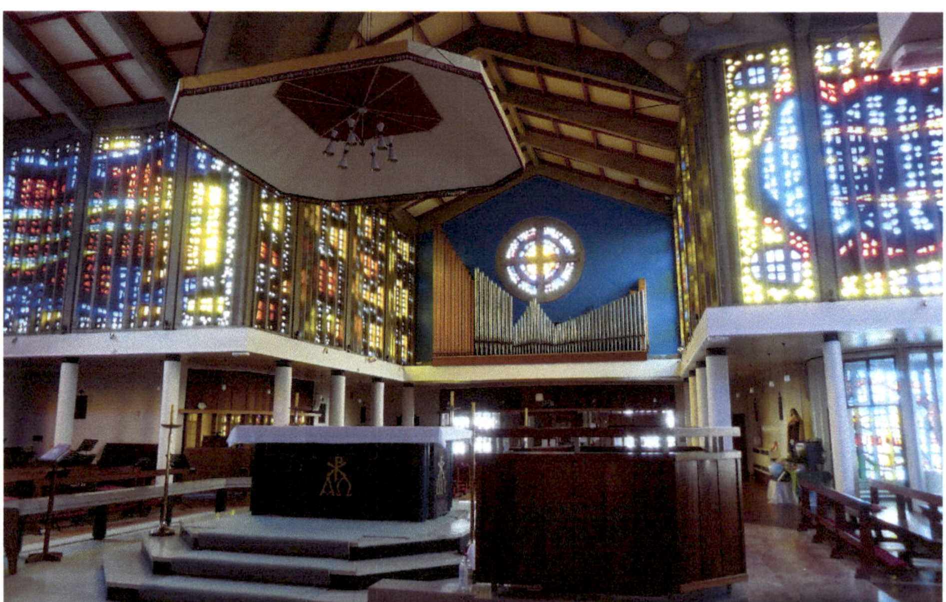

Interior of Our Lady's Roman Catholic Church, built in 1963 to the designs of local architect Henry Fedeski and filled with dazzlingly colourful *dalle-de-verre* glazing.

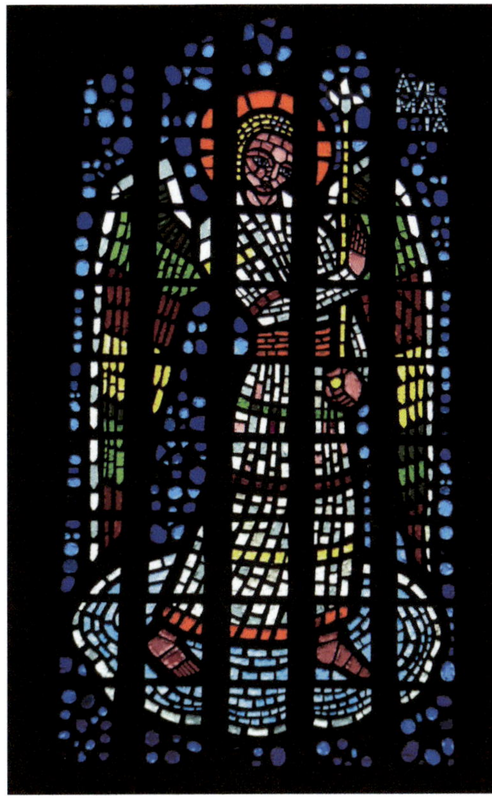

Transept window in rich *dalle-de-verre* glass, designed by Dom Charles Norris of Buckfast. The huge figure of Archangel Gabriel is balanced by a figure of Mary opposite to create an Annunciation across the transepts.

The brilliant glass is the work of Dom Charles Norris of Buckfast, heading a team of monks who employed the *dalle-de-verre* ('slab of glass') technique, wherein thick chunks of coloured glass are set in a concrete matrix, manifesting externally as a busy concrete lattice while exuding deep colour within. The entire clerestory of all four arms of the building consists of this rich abstract glazing, resulting in complete walls of glowing colour. A round window pierces the entrance façade and peers over the organ within (liturgically west facing but the church is actually orientated north to south) while the transepts are dominated by huge images of Mary and the Archangel Gabriel, respectively (the only figurative elements in the glazing). There are yet further examples of this rich glass at ground level in two side chapels and the circular baptistry, all making a visit to this church an unforgettable experience.

35. Lower Shuckburgh, St John the Baptist

A rural Victorian church worthy of inclusion, if only for its sheer eccentricity. This is a complete rebuilding from 1864 of the previous medieval church by John Croft, one of the so-called 'rogue architects' of the era who veered away from the more historically inspired forms of their contemporaries, in this case introducing Moorish elements into the design of an otherwise Gothic church (believed to have been influenced by Sir George Shuckburgh after returning from Crimea).

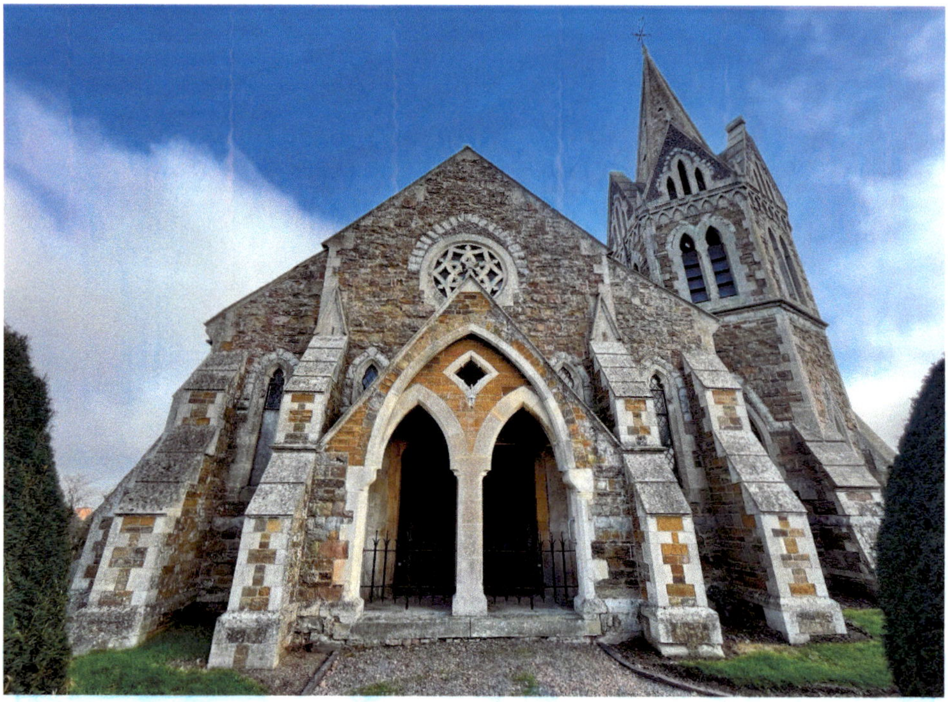

The west front of the idiosyncratic St John the Baptist Church of 1864 designed by John Croft. Note the flat tracery of the rose window and the 'Moorish' arches of the belfry windows in the hexagonal steeple.

However it may break the rules, it is hard not to be charmed by the quirkiness of this building, with its strangely designed windows and unusual hexagonal south-west tower, also serving as a porch with a vaulted ceiling within. The interior contrasts with the two-toned stonework outside by being finished in brick and plaster, culminating in the attractive vaulted chancel finished in brick and tile. The simple furnishings are original to the church's rebuilding (aside from the ancient font from its predecessor) and there is no stained glass, leaving us free to focus on this delightful architectural oddity.

36. Mancetter, St Peter

Mancetter began as a Roman settlement on Watling Street and a possible site of the final defeat of Queen Boudica in AD 60, celebrated today with an exhibition in the south aisle of the church. The church itself is an impressive thirteenth- to fourteenth-century building consisting of nave with spacious aisles and a long and well-lit chancel. The sturdy but low west tower of contrasting red sandstone was finished a century later, while the south porch was rebuilt in brick in the late seventeenth century.

The broad interior lightens eastwards thanks to the well-glazed chancel, culminating in the church's chief feature of interest, an east window filled with a patchwork collection of fragments of medieval glass. The ancient glass here

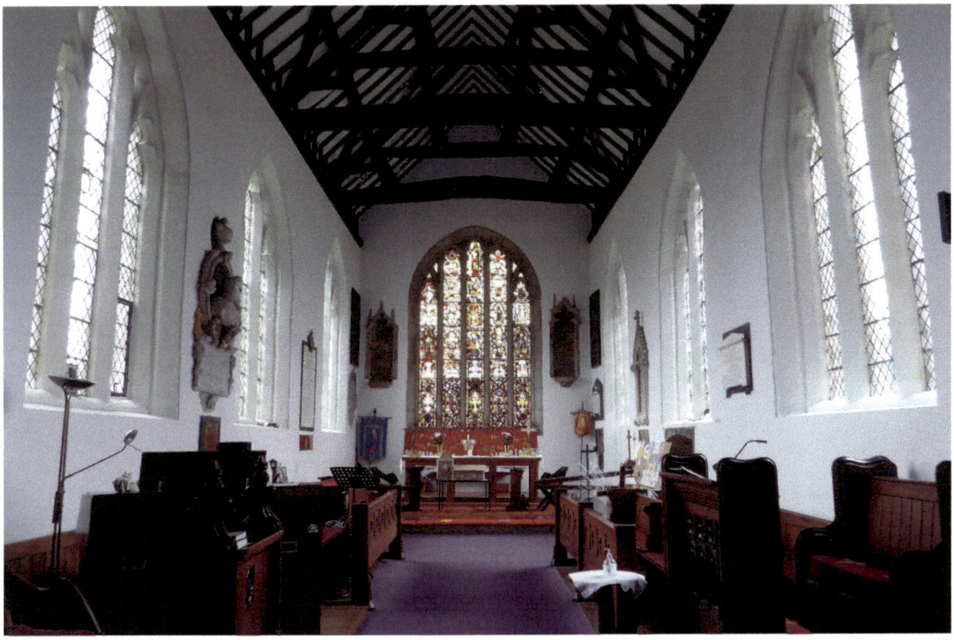

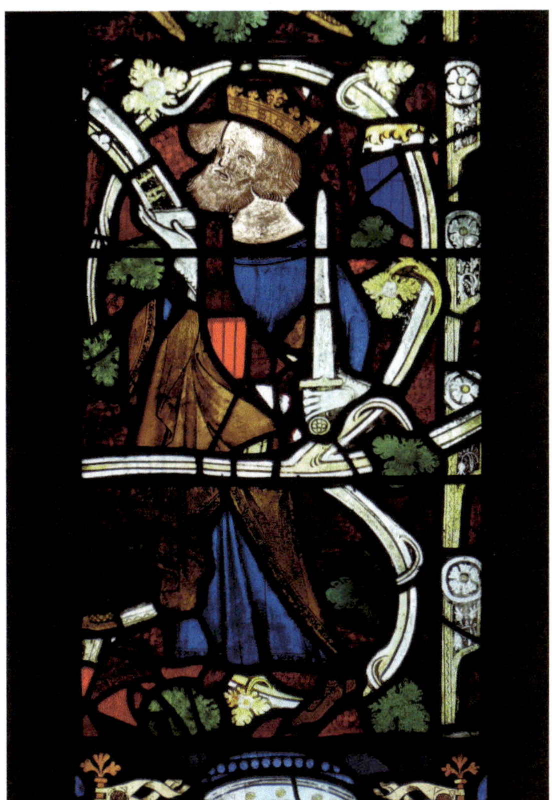

Above: View of St Peter's Church's fourteenth-century chancel, pleasingly light from an abundance of generously sized windows. The glass in the east window is a patchwork of mostly fourteenth-century glass from various windows in the church.

Right: A fourteenth-century king from a Jesse Tree, part of the collection of medieval glass in the east window. Three such figures are traditionally believed to originate from nearby Merevale Abbey where a more complete set remains, but stylistic comparison suggests they are unrelated and more likely original to Mancetter's church.

belongs mainly to the fourteenth and century, though there are late fifteenth-century canopies and later pieces, along with Victorian material augmenting the lower panels. The three finest figures in the central light are from a Jesse Tree and popularly thought to originate from nearby Merevale Abbey, but various differences in execution from the glass still at Merevale suggest they are far more likely original to this church. The surrounding figures in quatrefoils certainly seem compatible with the east window tracery of the north aisle here. A fine fifteenth-century head can also be seen in one of the north facing windows.

Also in the chancel is a fine late seventeenth-century memorial with a portrait bust to Edward Hinton (d. 1689), while memorial boards of 1833 to the Mancetter martyrs of the 1550s flank the organ at the west end. Nearby a quirky eighteenth-century royal arms shows lion and unicorn bizarrely reduced to a pair of slightly comical heads.

37. Merevale, Our Lady

Set in a quiet enclave hidden behind a Victorian gatehouse, Merevale is one of Warwickshire's most unique medieval churches, a rarity having originally served as the gate chapel ('cappella ante portas') to adjacent Merevale Abbey, once a major Cistercian monastery but now mostly vanished, its few remnants incorporated into neighbouring Abbey Farm.

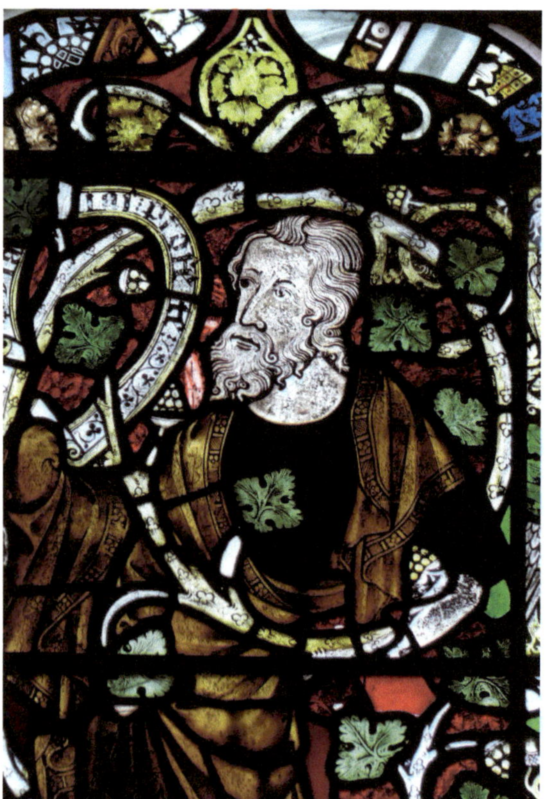

Church of Our Lady, Merevale. Prophet Isaiah in fourteenth-century glass, part of the sequence of prophets and kings from a Jesse Tree in the east window, believed to have originated from a window in the now lost abbey church and found buried in the grounds centuries later.

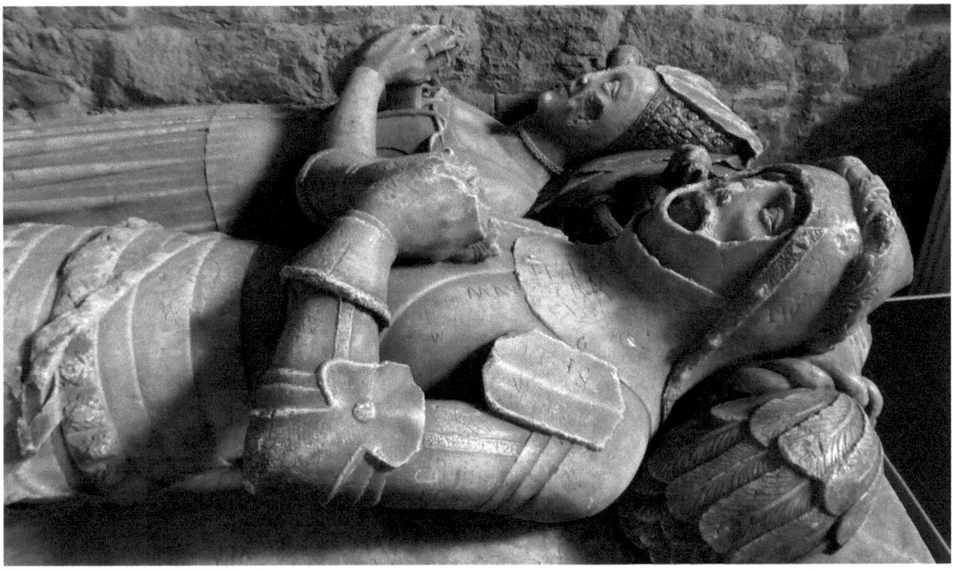

Alabaster effigies of a fifteenth-century knight and lady, presumed to be members of the Ferrers family.

The church has a most unusual layout, with a short two-bay nave (its aisles long ago demolished) followed by a far grander four-bay Perpendicular chancel with aisles, a reversal of the usual parish church layout. A simple wooden bell turret with a tiny spire pierces the roof. The dark and mysterious interior is one of the most memorable in the county and full of interest.

There are fine medieval monuments: a tomb with alabaster effigies of a knight and lady of the Ferrers family, a headless thirteenth-century knight and a superb pair of brasses of Robert Earl Ferrers (d. 1412) and his wife Margaret. The fifteenth-century former rood screen with a projecting central balcony remarkably retains its loft and is now relocated at the west end.

The outstanding feature, however, is the ancient glass, principally the fine series of prophets and kings from *c.* 1320 in the east window, remains of a Jesse Tree believed to have come from the abbey. It was found buried nearby in the early nineteenth century and subsequently restored; its lower figures are largely clever reproductions, but much of the rest is genuine and of high quality. In the aisle windows are further fragments of fourteenth- and sixteenth-century glass original to this building.

38. Middleton, St John the Baptist

One of north Warwickshire's more enjoyable churches, its origin is Norman as witnessed by the chevron-decorated south door concealed within an eighteenth-century brick porch. The rest is a mixture of thirteenth-century work in a lighter stone with early sixteenth-century Perpendicular additions and modifications in red sandstone, with a handsome west tower and walls heightened to allow clerestory windows.

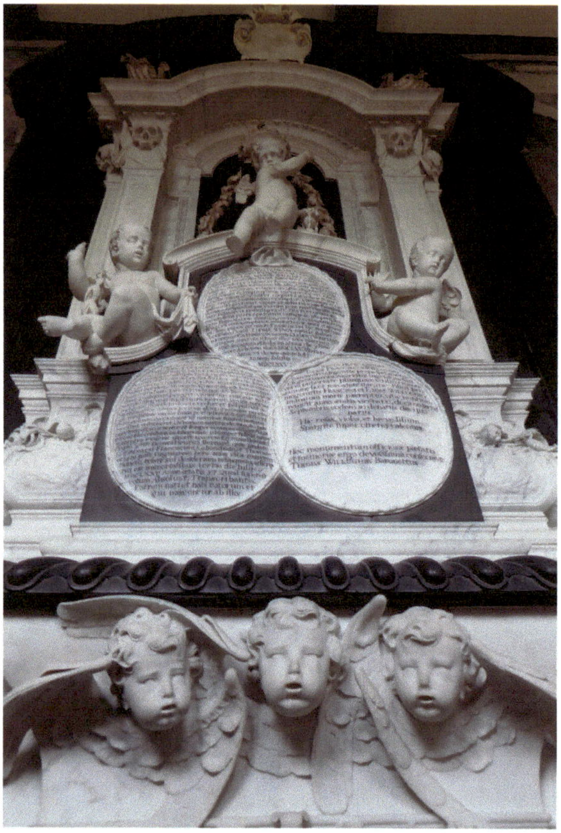

St John the Baptist's Church, Middleton. The exuberant marble monument on the north side of the chancel to Francis Willoughby (d. 1675) and other members of the Willoughby family, surrounded by cherubs and putti.

The interior is somewhat asymmetric, with only a northern side aisle and an off-centre chancel arch still framing its fine fifteenth-century wooden screen (carvings include a green man and a leonine face). The chancel beyond contains several interesting memorials, earliest of which are the fine late medieval brasses Sir Richard Bingham (d. 1476) and his wife. Of the three notable seventeenth-century monuments, the best is the towering white-marble confection on the north wall adorned with quite animated putti, commemorating members of the Willoughby family.

It is worth exploring the north aisle for the patchy remains of thirteenth-century wall paintings discovered only recently: remnants of figures executed in red on white, allowing a small glimpse of how iconographically rich pre-Reformation interiors must have been.

39. Monks Kirby, St Edith

One of the grandest churches in Warwickshire, having once served a Benedictine priory founded in 1077 (of which nothing else remains). It was built on an impressive scale, the aisled nave and chancel form one vessel with no structural division, all built of rich red sandstone except for the later upper part of the tower, giving it a distinctive two-toned red and white look. The mighty tower once carried a spire which fell in 1701, after which the present parapet was added.

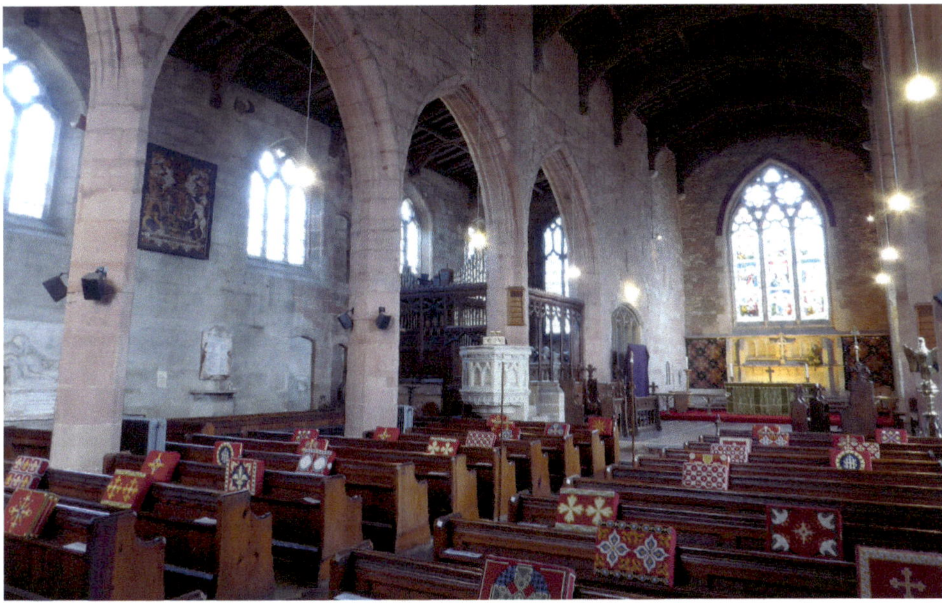

Interior of the former priory church at Monks Kirby, showing the unusually elevated windows of the north aisle, suggesting room was left for a cloister beneath. The enclosed north-east chapel contains the Tudor period Feilding tombs.

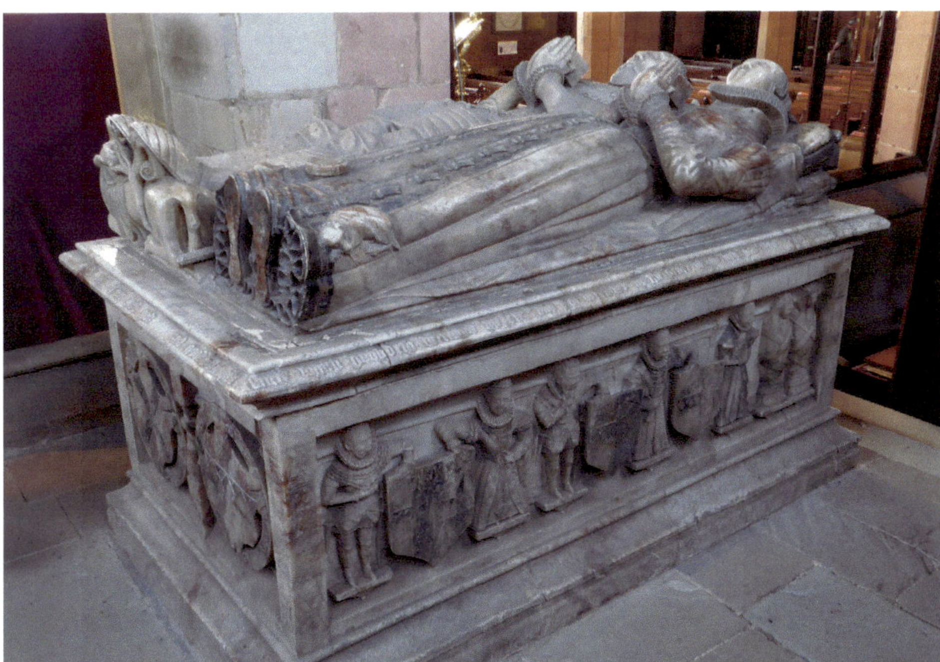

Tomb of Basil Feilding and his wife Gooddethe (d. 1580) in the north chapel. Both the alabaster tombs here are the work of Garrat Hollemans of Burton-upon-Trent.

The interior is a huge, cavernous space with all three aisles of a similar height, its gloom is warmed by the pinkness of the stonework. The windows on the north side are high up, presumably to permit a now vanished cloister beneath them. Both the tower and south porch have fine rib-vaulted ceilings, an extravagance for a village church but not a formerly monastic one. The furnishings are mostly of the Victorian period as is the rich glass, most of it by Hardman aside from a fine east window by Lavers & Barraud.

Of more interest are the monuments, with two Tudor-period tombs with effigies of William and Basil Fielding with their wives in the north chapel. Both are from the Burton-upon-Trent alabaster workshops and illustrate a transition from medieval to Elizabethan design and costume. Further along the aisle are ghostly white marble nineteenth-century memorials with members of the Earl of Denbigh's family in high relief, while a badly worn medieval knight's head (and lost effigy fragment) pokes alarmingly out of the wall at the west end.

40. Newbold-on-Avon, St Botolph

Though now a suburb of Rugby, St Botolph's Church sits in a lush churchyard on the edge of the countryside so preserves a more rural feel. The handsome tower and nave date from the fifteenth century along with the north porch, which is adorned with niches; the chancel is an early Victorian replacement.

Within, the nave arcades are lofty and elegant with pillars of an unusual design. The interior is light thanks to the nave clerestory and Victorian stained glass being

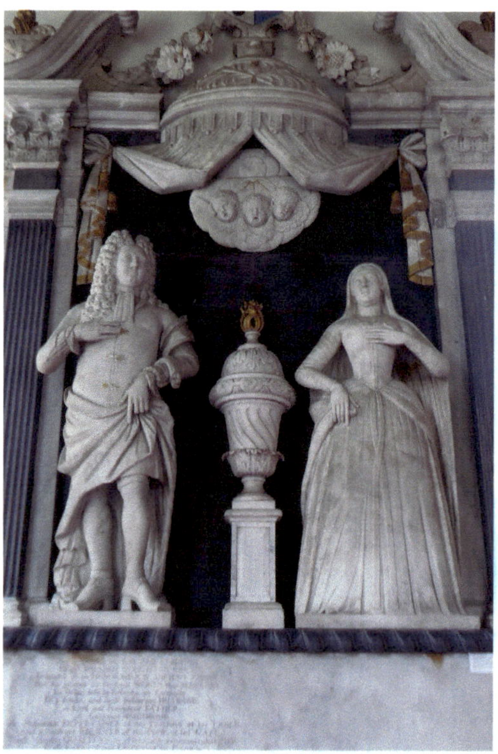

Baroque monument at St Botolph's Church on the south side of the chancel to Sir William Boughton and his wife, the work of John Hunt of Northampton, 1716.

confined to the nave aisles – three windows by Heaton, Butler & Bayne on the north side, one by Burlison & Grylls to the south.

The monuments here are of particular interest and from distinct periods. The earliest group are in the south aisle, consisting of two mid-fifteenth-century tombs with flat incised slabs depicting Geoffrey Allesley and Thomas Boughton with their respective wives, the latter images being much better preserved. Also here are two painted alabaster wall monuments carved with small, rather folksy figures in relief to two generations of the Boughton family (one Elizabethan, the other Jacobean). The largest memorial of all is that to William Boughton and wife from 1716, a rather pompous baroque showpiece in white marble with standing figures that dominates the chancel.

41. Nuneaton, St Nicholas

St Nicholas' provides the sort of landmark architecture Nuneaton sorely needs, though is unfortunately somewhat marginalised by the ring road, separating it from the rest of the town centre. The embattled tower of grey local stone (like the rest of the church) nevertheless does its best to assert its presence.

The eastern parts are still largely fourteenth-century Decorated work, but most of the present building dates from the following century. It is a grand Perpendicular church with an aisled nave crowned by clerestories (inside spanned

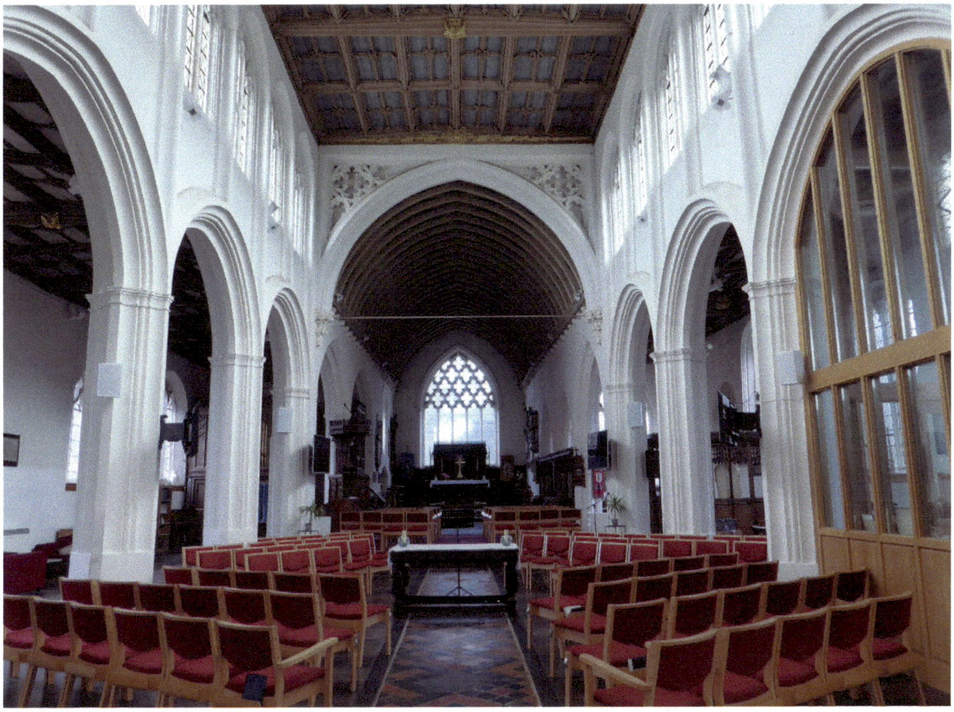

The attractive fifteenth-century nave of St Nicholas' Church, Nuneaton, with its original flat-panelled ceiling. The interior here remains light owing to the wartime loss of most of the Victorian stained glass.

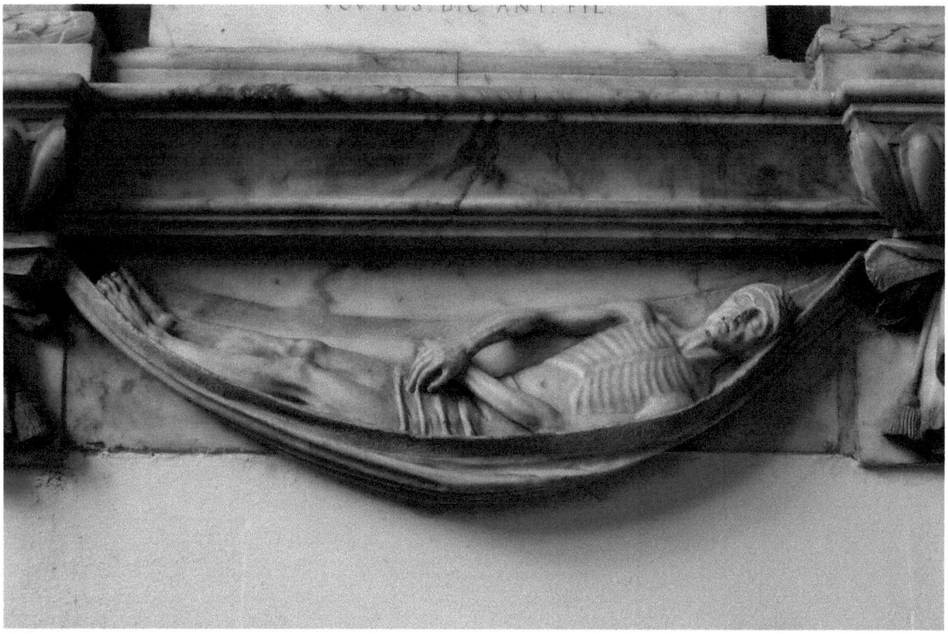

Detail from the Anthony Trotman memorial from 1703, showing the deceased as a corpse suspended in a hammock-like shroud.

by the original gorgeous panelled ceiling). The eccentrically staggered windows of the south chapel are a testament to the extensive fifteenth-century modifications.

The attractive interior is impressive, elegant and very light, owing to whitewashed walls and a lack of stained glass (all the Victorian glass was destroyed by wartime bombing, excepting one window in the south chapel). Both nave and aisles are crowned by exceedingly handsome late medieval panelled ceilings studded with bosses, mostly foliage carvings with a few isolated heads (most notably the grinning faces at the west end). The chancel is mostly a rebuilding of 1852, but it is here that the most interesting memorials are to be found. On the north side lies the effigy of Sir Marmaduke Constable (d. 1560), who converted nearby Nuneaton Abbey into his mansion following the Dissolution. Opposite is the handsome baroque Trotman Memorial from 1703, with busts of the deceased couple and a forlorn-looking corpse in a winding sheet below.

Nuneaton, St Mary

North-west of the town centre is St Mary's Abbey, or perhaps more accurately the church built upon its ruins. All that remains of the former Benedictine nunnery (founded *c.* 1150) are the hefty crossing piers now incorporated into the present cruciform church built in three phases upon the old foundations between 1876 and 1930. The church had been converted into a mansion after the Dissolution, which itself was abandoned in later centuries allowing the Victorian revival of the site, though the rebuilding was never completed, thus the south transept and western half of the nave remain ruined fragments.

42. Oxhill, St Lawrence

Oxhill sits in the pleasant countryside of south Warwickshire and its fine old church shows the delightful effect of the local honey-coloured ironstone patinated with a sprinkling of silvery lichen. It dates back to Norman times and structurally largely remains of this period, though the windows are mostly later alterations and additions from the fourteenth and fifteenth centuries. The best feature is the Romanesque doorway on the south side, as its Norman sculptors left it, albeit a little weathered by time.

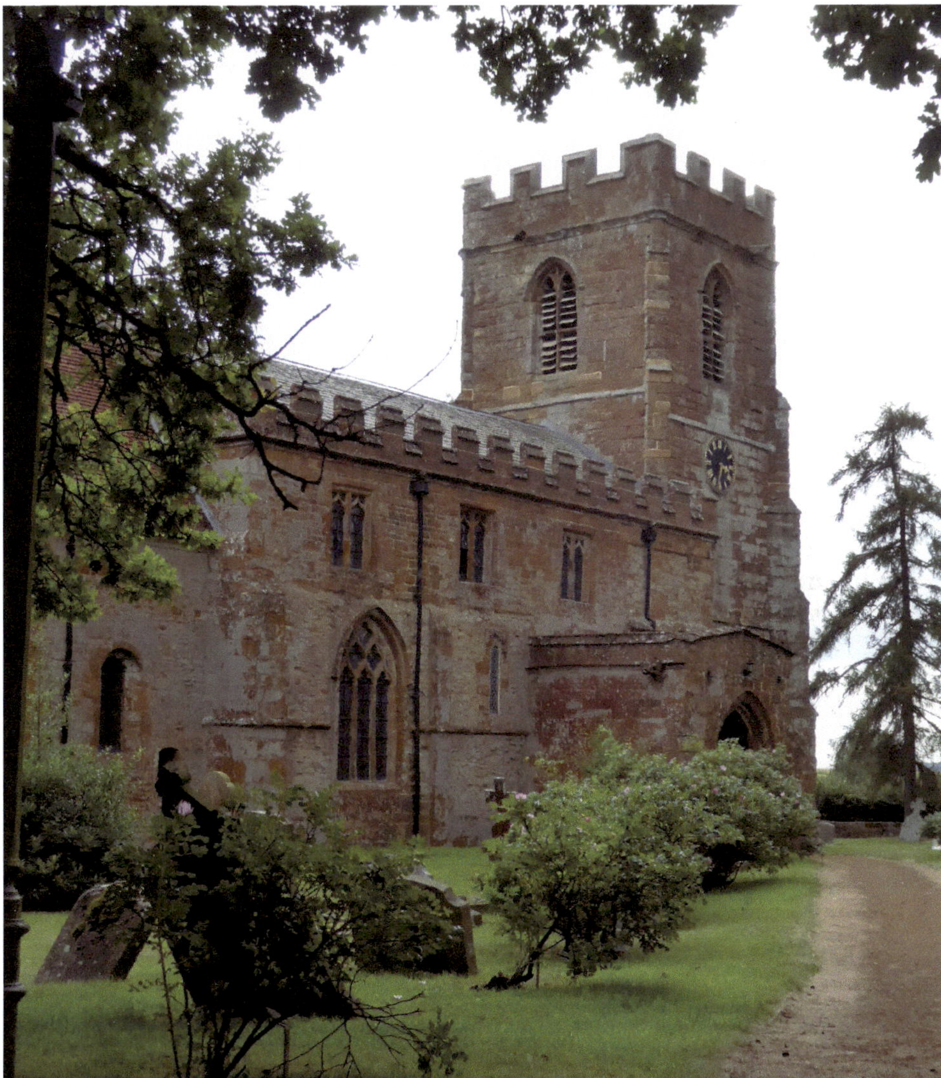

View from the north-east of the largely Norman St Lawrence's Church, Oxhill, where one original window can be seen alongside a much-enlarged fourteenth-century one. A horizontal line marks where the walls were raised in the fifteenth century to accommodate the clerestory.

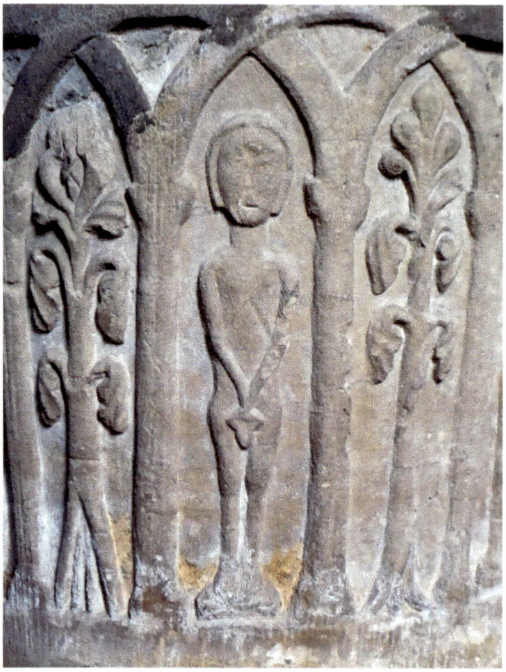

Detail of the carved Norman font, which includes separate figures of poor Adam and Eve looking very embarrassed about their nudity as they cling to their fig leaves!

The interior is clean and simple and flooded with light with no stained glass to subdue this, thanks also to the clerestory added in the fifteenth century, about the same time as the present tower was built. There is medieval woodwork in the benches at the west end, some of which have traceried panels on the ends.

The most memorable item here, however, is the Norman font with its carved decoration, mostly foliate designs in arched-recesses but also including primitive figures representing Adam and Eve, each very self-consciously clutching a fig leaf to conceal their nether regions!

43. Packwood, St Giles

Tucked away in a quiet corner close to Packwood House, this handsome medieval church is every bit as rewarding. The outstanding feature of the exterior is the handsome battlemented fifteenth-century tower (similar in design to that at nearby Baddesley Clinton) which greets the visitor. The rest of the building comprises thirteenth-century nave and chancel with an eighteenth-century north transept in brick, built as a mortuary chapel.

Inside it can take a moment to adjust to the low light level, but the eye is drawn towards the curiously low chancel arch, around which are remains of a fifteenth-century painting showing the 'Three Living and the Dead' – three figures in costly garments encountering three skeletons, now mostly faded, a reminder of man's mortality then popular in art. The small chancel beyond is a lighter space that still retains a few fragments of ancient glass, though so heavily corroded to be difficult to discern. The stunning east window by Richard Stubington draws focus here, a dramatic composition of the dead Christ on the Cross with a seated angel below

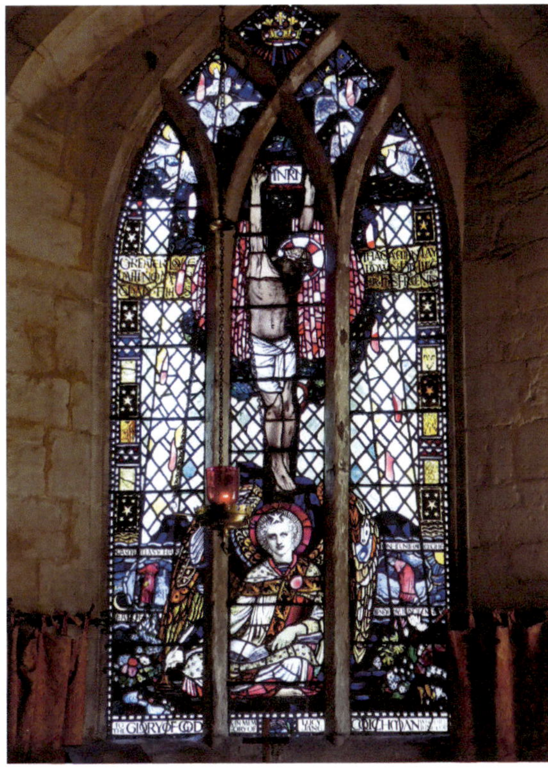

St Giles' Church, Packwood. The striking 1914 Arts and Crafts east window by Richard Stubington, representing the dying Christ with an Angel of Remembrance holding a book below, engaging the viewer with his gaze.

engaging the viewer, a beautiful example of Arts and Crafts glass (as is the small Theodora Salusbury window in the nave depicting the Holy Family and signed with an exuberant peacock).

The north chapel contains another stained-glass Crucifixion but a much earlier one dating from the fourteenth century, while the walls here are adorned with some richly ornamented eighteenth-century memorials replete with cherubs and grisly skulls.

44. Polesworth, St Edith

The former Polesworth Abbey was once part of a Benedictine nunnery, believed to have been founded in *c.* 827. It is approached from the north via a picturesque half-timbered gate house and a tree-lined lane. The church beyond is dominated by the heavy mass of the sturdy tower on the north side and consists of the nave and north aisle of the old abbey church with a small Victorian chancel beyond. The old cloister stood on the south side where some remains are still visible.

The spacious interior immediately impresses with the Norman north arcade and former clerestory and north aisle of almost equal proportions to the nave. The arcade itself was largely rebuilt in Victorian times (during a rather thorough restoration by G. E. Street in 1868) but sensitively copies the Norman work at the east end. The old chancel appears to have been lost after the Dissolution, thus the present one is an entirely Victorian addition.

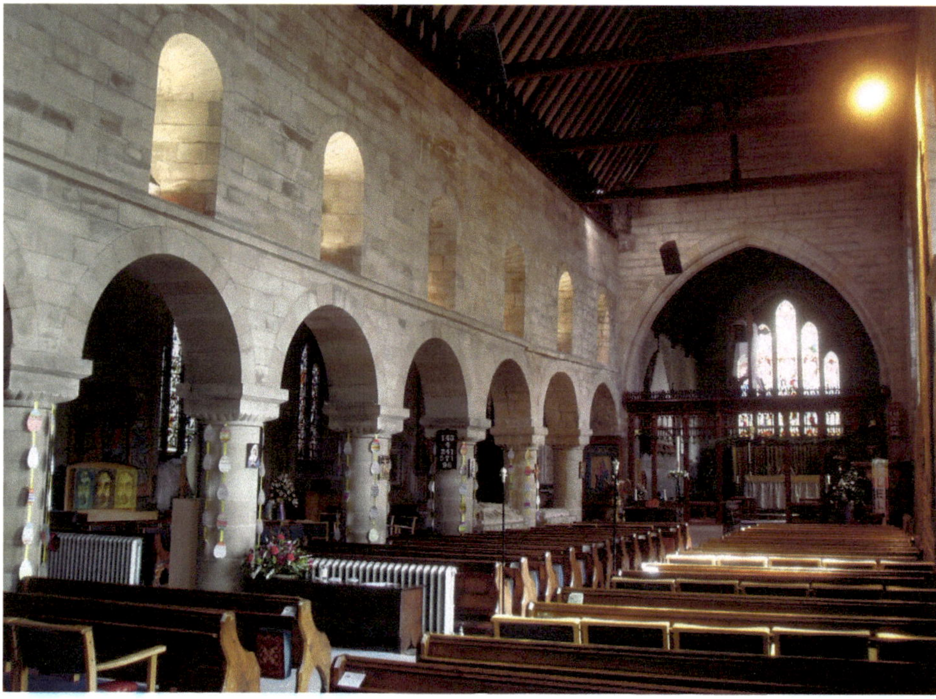

View of the nave of the abbey showing the genuine Norman north arcade, whose eastern parts are original (the rest is a careful reconstruction by George Edmund Street from 1868).

Aside from the fourteenth-century font the furnishings too are mostly Victorian, along with the stained glass (the rich east window by Clayton & Bell). There are two fine medieval tombs under the arcade, one with an alabaster effigy of a fifteenth-century lady, the other an abbess's effigy in low relief from *c.* 1200, lying atop an otherwise unrelated fifteenth-century tomb-chest.

45. Preston on Stour, St Mary

A little-known gem of a church, the tower and nave are largely late medieval but with significant remodelling in 1753–57 by Edward Woodward of Chipping Campden, who originally planned a much more ambitious replacement. The chancel was entirely rebuilt at this time, though the blend of old and new is surprisingly homogenous.

The light and pleasant interior is full of interest, mostly inside the chancel which has a series of wall-mounted monuments of seventeenth- and eighteenth-century date. The earliest of these shows Nicholas Kempe (d. 1624) kneeling between his two wives, while the later memorials are carefully organised within ogee-arched Gothic panels on either side.

The stained glass takes centre stage, however, with a magnificent collection of Continental roundels in the east window, mostly depicting Old and New Testament subjects but including fascinating allegories of Death and Purity – the central Christ figure is a 1904 imposition by Powell's; what was there before? On either side are

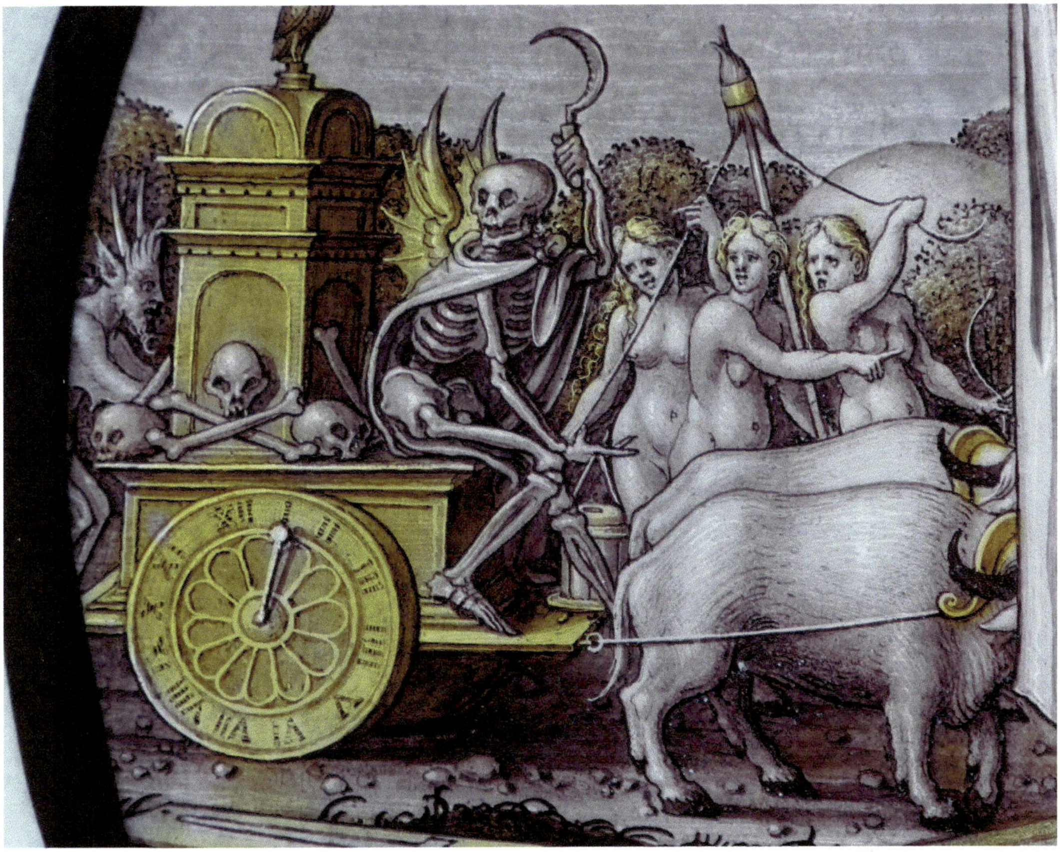

An allegory of Death mounted on the Chariot of Time and followed by the Devil, a detail of one of the sixteenth-century Continental roundels in the east window at St Mary's, Preston on Stour.

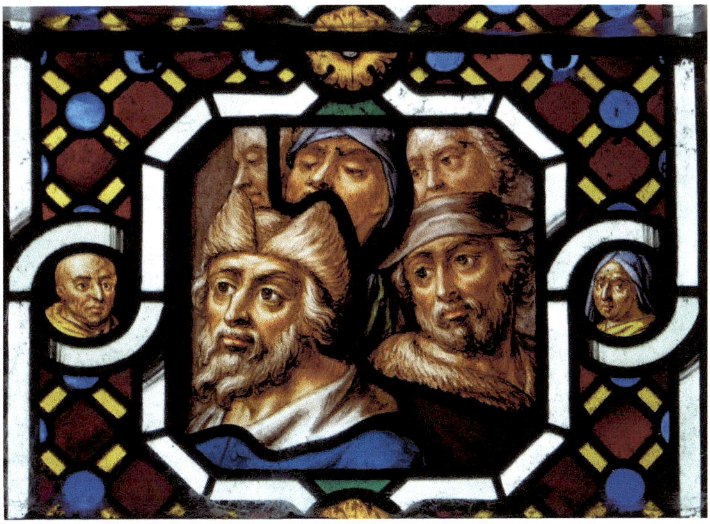

One of the colourful portrait medallions by William Price the Younger in the side windows of the chancel, an eccentric display designed to complement the antiquarian collection in the east window at St Mary's.

two superb and extremely unusual side windows by William Price the Younger from the 1750s, with standing saints flanked by an eccentric collection of portrait medallions, designed to appear as another antiquarian collection replete with neo-medieval elements but all of a piece (Price having assembled the east window, apparently 'colouring in' a few pieces with enamel during the process).

There is a further assemblage of notable earlier glass in the west window under the tower, largely comprising early sixteenth-century work, much perhaps original to the church (though sadly difficult to see without special access to the bell-ringing chamber).

46. Quinton, St Swithin

This stately church is one of the most impressive in south-west Warwickshire, with a handsome exterior and much of interest to reward the visitor. The building owes its present appearance largely to fourteenth-century rebuilding and extension, culminating in the upper part of the tower with its elegant spire, both fifteenth-century additions in contrastingly light limestone. Its origins, however, are much earlier, as witnessed inside by late twelfth-century round arches of the south nave arcade.

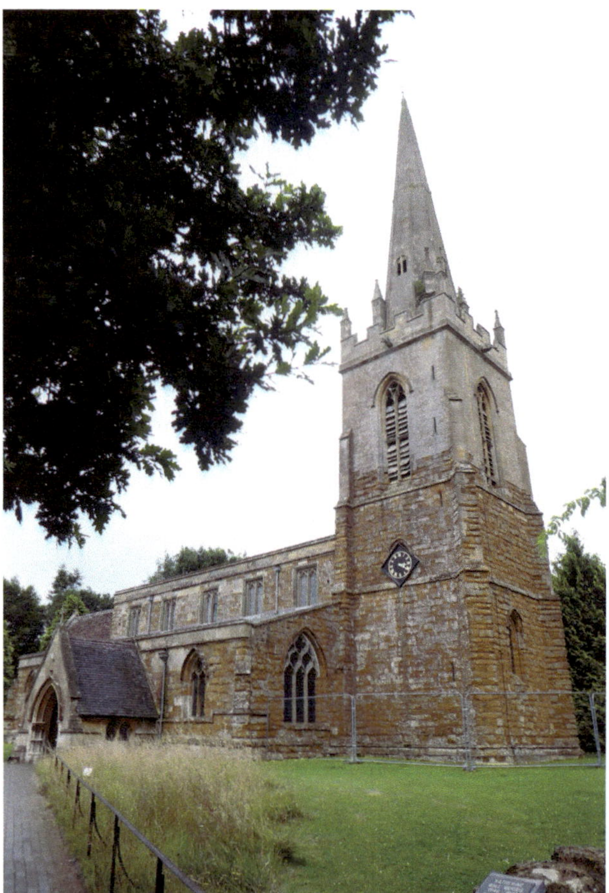

View from the north-west showing the largely fourteenth-century exterior of St Swithin's in ironstone with the later fifteenth-century tower and spire completed in paler limestone.

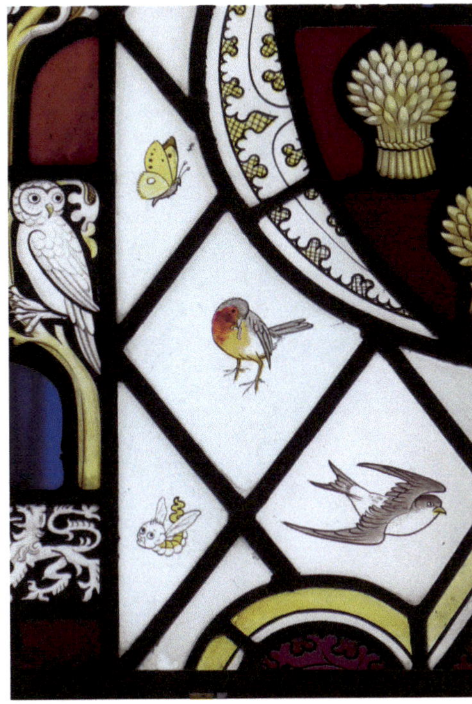

Detail of one of the aisle windows by Geoffrey Webb from *c.* 1930, with heraldic glass surrounded by charming quarries of birds and whimsical creatures.

The interior immediately shows its layers of history. The nave arcades are low and early with much solid masonry between them and the clerestory above. Beneath one of the arches lies a knight's effigy (Sir William Clopton, d. 1419) and above the chancel arch is a damaged mural of the royal arms of Elizabeth I. At the east end of the south aisle below a handsome baroque tablet is a fifteenth-century tomb-chest with a fine brass to Lady Joanna Clopton (d. 1430). The font is Norman with simple scalloped decoration.

There are fragments of medieval glass in several windows on the north side, but most of the glazing is attractive early twentieth-century work by Geoffrey Webb (mostly heraldic, with some delightful tiny birds and whimsical creatures in one window). The east window is Victorian and both its stonework and glass are the work of Frederick Preedy, who restored the church in 1864.

47. Rugby, St Andrew

This church makes the grade for sheer spectacle and most unusually possesses two towers. The original fifteenth-century battlemented one is at the west end and the mighty Victorian steeple by William Butterfield to the north-east, part of his rebuilding of the ancient church. The medieval church had already been greatly altered; originally a village church, it was gradually expanded in the 1800s to serve the growing town. When Butterfield further enlarged the building in 1877–85 only the west tower and the north nave arcade survived of the medieval building. These were retained, the old nave effectively becoming the north aisle (with an outer north aisle) of a much larger nave with its own south aisle and lofty chancel.

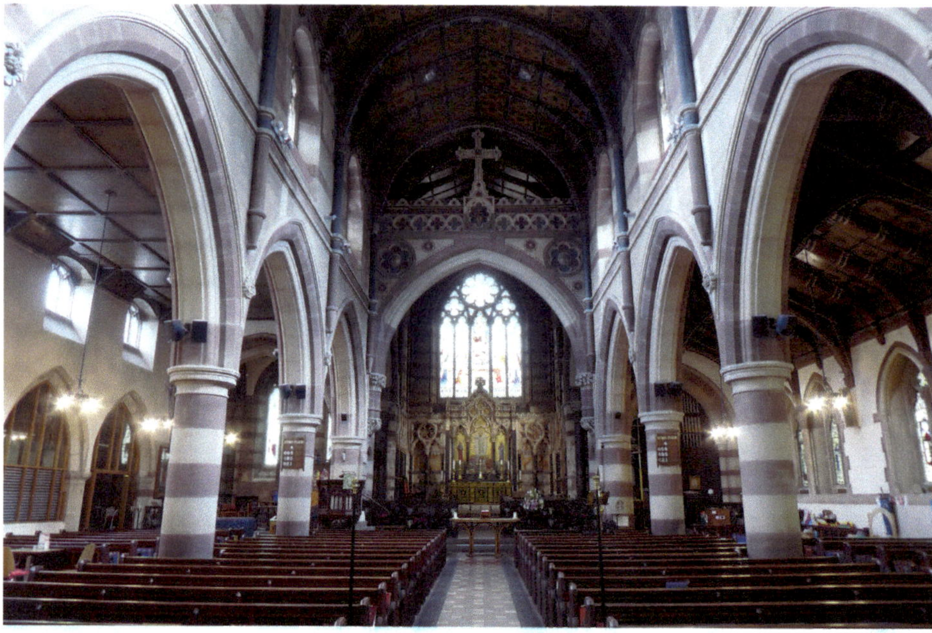

The impressively proportioned nave of St Andrew's by William Butterfield, added in 1877–85 to the medieval building whose original nave then became the north aisle (its remaining north arcade visible lower left).

The interior is every bit as eccentric as the exterior, with Butterfield's characteristic use of coloured stonework and a sanctuary rich in marble finishes. The most dramatic feature is the chancel arch surmounted by a cross adorned with geometric patterning and supported by richly carved corbels. The font too betrays Butterfield's love of contrasting coloured marbles and a fragment of its medieval predecessor remains.

The stained glass in the main east and west windows (along with the flanking sanctuary windows) is by Clayton & Bell. The rest is all the work of Burlison & Grylls, with their characteristic neo-Flemish fine drawing and subdued tones.

Rugby, St Marie

As unusual as Rugby's two-towered church is with its complex building history, remarkably the nearby Roman Catholic church evolved in a strikingly similar way; thus, both major churches here uniquely each possess an asymmetrical pair of towers. St Marie's began as a small building with a saddle-backed tower designed by A. W. N. Pugin and finished in 1847 but greatly expanded to its north by his son Edward Pugin twenty years later, so that the old church now serves as the south aisle and chapel to the new nave and apse. Finally, a soaring steeple was added in 1872, a splendid showpiece that dwarfs its diminutive Pugin-designed predecessor. The interior is also impressive, colourful and richly adorned with much glass by Hardman and others and an elaborate altar reredos.

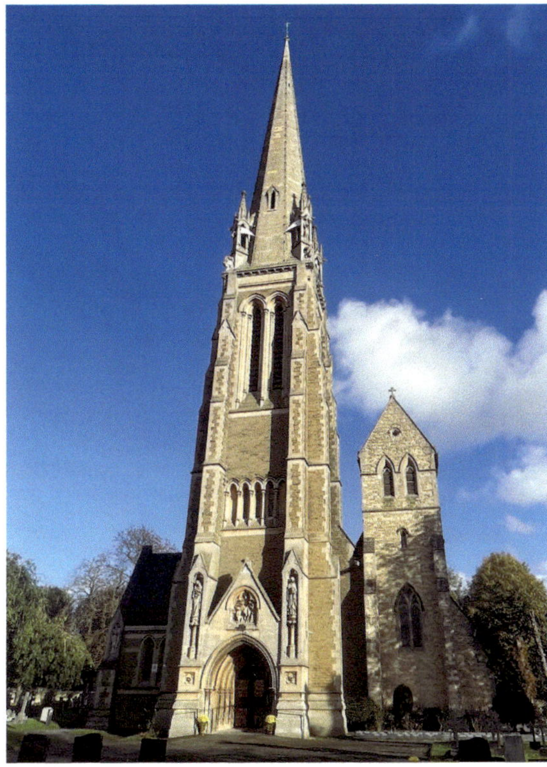

The impressive steeple of Rugby's main Roman Catholic church was added by Bernard Whelan in 1872. It completely dwarfs the modest saddle-backed tower of A. W. N. Pugin's original church of 1847.

48. Rugby, School Chapel

Rugby School Chapel is a gloriously eccentric piece of Victorian architecture, one of the most ambitious buildings by William Butterfield, an architect renowned for his love of polychrome brickwork whose work is a defining feature of the town, mostly in various parts of the school complex.

The previous chapel was a much more modest affair, Butterfield's rebuilding in 1872 being on a far grander scale, culminating in the distinctive octagonal tower above that has become such a landmark of the school since. Initially the nave of the old chapel was retained when the new transepts, tower and apse were built, but this was later rebuilt in a style more in keeping with the rest of the building by Thomas Jackson in 1897–98 (with the elderly Butterfield's assistance). The chapel has thus retained a more unified appearance inside and out ever since.

The chapel is an architectural delight inside and out, and first stepping into the rich polychrome interior is a memorable experience – Victorian architectural confectionery at its best. What makes a visit all the more rewarding is the richly varied collection of stained glass, a surprising mixture encompassing Northern Renaissance to late Pre-Raphaelite. Four windows contain early sixteenth-century Continental glass imported in the early nineteenth century (originally installed in the old chapel). The finest is the Flemish glass in the east window depicting the Adoration of the Magi, originating from the abbey of Aerschot near Louvain (from the same source a north nave window depicting the risen Christ appearing

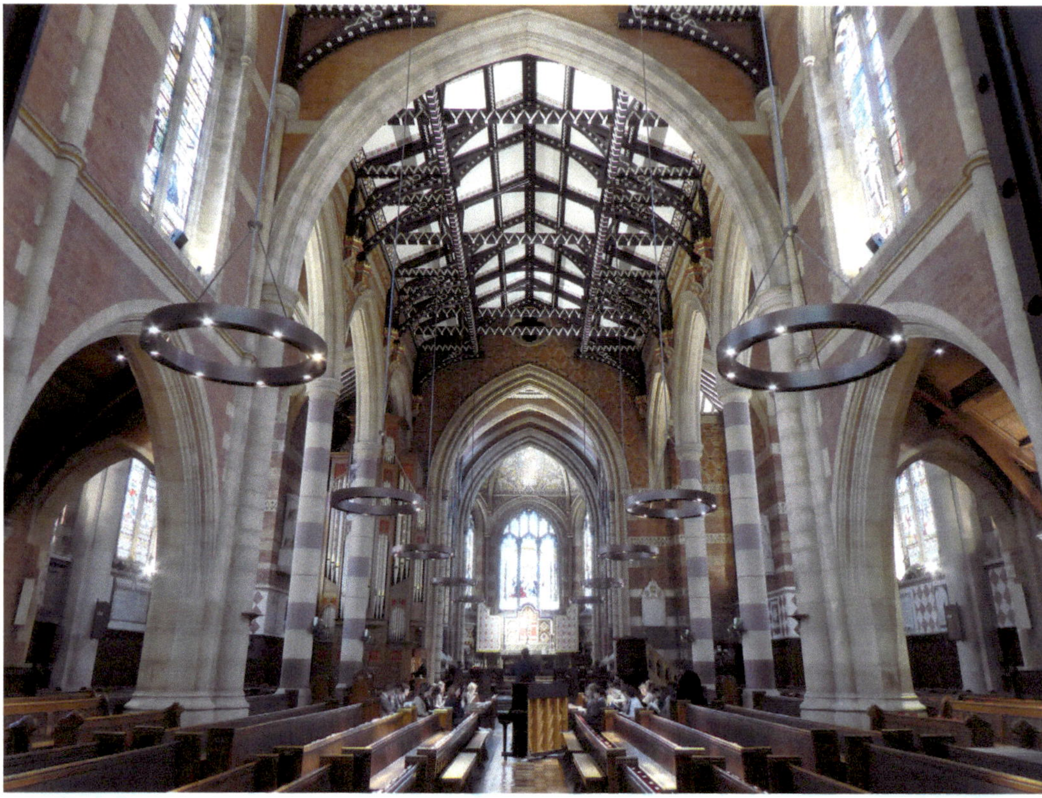

The stunning interior of William Butterfield's Rugby School Chapel, rebuilt in 1872 using a mixture of stone and polychrome brickwork. The nave in the foreground is a later addition of 1897–98 designed to blend with Butterfield's work.

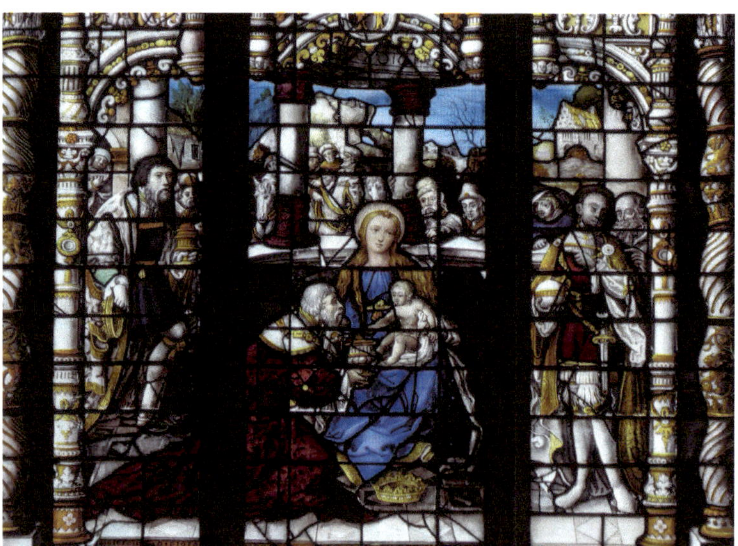

Detail of the east window with an Adoration of the Magi in sixteenth-century Flemish glass from the abbey of Aerschot near Louvain and given to the school in 1834 (Mary's head is a nineteenth-century restoration).

to Mary). There is much Victorian glass by several makers, mainly Alexander Gibbs, who regularly worked with Butterfield and whose huge windows dominate the transepts in addition to the mosaic ceiling of the apse. The nave contains more compelling work, predominately late pieces by Morris & Co., including the stunning west window by J. H. Dearle.

At the west end a passageway with attractive trefoil rose windows (a remnant of the previous chapel) leads to the Memorial Chapel, a separate cruciform building designed by Sir Charles Nicholson erected in 1922. Its austere interior comes as a relief after the exuberance of the main chapel, but the late Burlison & Grylls windows add a pleasing touch of richness.

49. Salford Priors, St Matthew

Salford Priors feels like a county-border church; its stately tower in golden stone would look as much at home in Gloucestershire or south Worcestershire as Warwickshire. Its lower part is plain twelfth century with late fourteenth-century grandeur above.

The rest of the church reflects the same periods: early Perpendicular outside and a heavy transitional south arcade within. The chancel is restored Early English, the north nave wall largely Victorian but with a fine flowing Decorated window (copied by Preedy when he restored neighbouring Harvington Church in Worcestershire). There are some good medieval gargoyles on the south side,

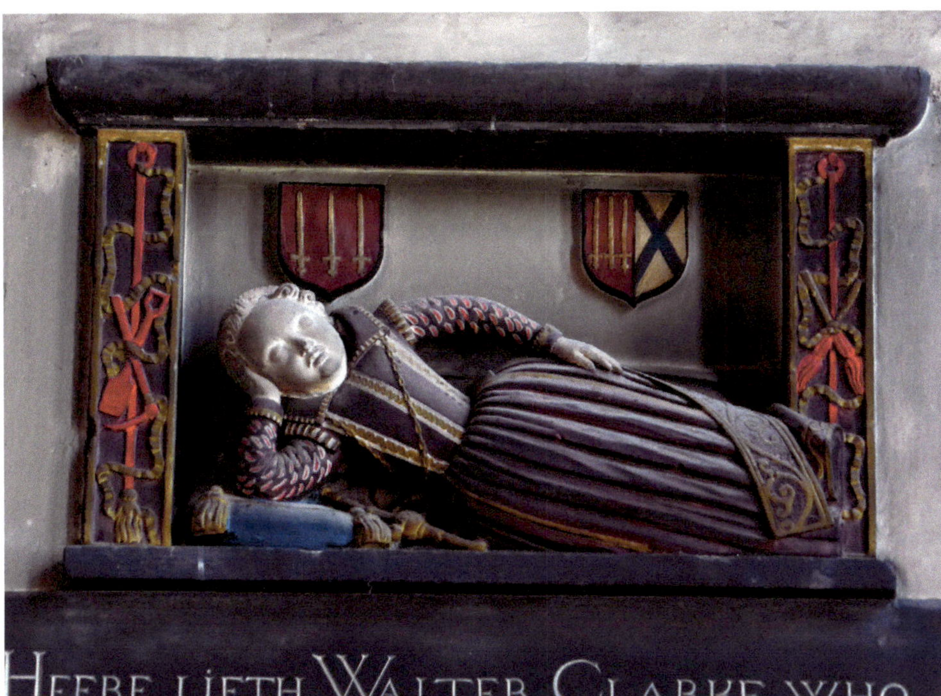

The tiny recumbent figure commemorating young Walter Clarke (d. 1607), strangely overshadowed by family heraldry at the heart of an immense wall tablet.

particularly on the surprisingly large octagonal stair turret, which is almost a second tower. A similar one is on the north side at Coughton, though shorn of its parapet. Too far west for a rood loft, its original function is unclear. The north porch has a Norman door with a patterned tympanum.

The interior feels more Victorian than it should thanks to the furnishings, the nave is light but of heavy proportions, while the chancel is alas too dark to fully appreciate the interesting seventeenth-century Clarke monuments that take up much of the wall space here (some to young children, one of whom is dwarfed by the surrounding display of family heraldry). There's a mixed bag of stained glass: some Victorian windows but also more attractive Arts and Crafts-inspired work in the chancel. Yet more pieces are inserted in the modern screens at the west end, salvaged from the demolished All Saints' in Warwick.

50. Sherbourne, All Saints

All Saints' at Sherbourne is a Victorian masterpiece by Sir George Gilbert Scott and probably the finest nineteenth-century village church in the county. It was built in 1862–64 with generous funding from local landowner Louisa Ryland, which allowed Gilbert Scott to spare no expense on the decoration within (such as the marble nave columns).

The interior is richly furnished and largely as Mrs Ryland and Gilbert Scott left it, with the addition of a south chapel containing a memorial to the founder

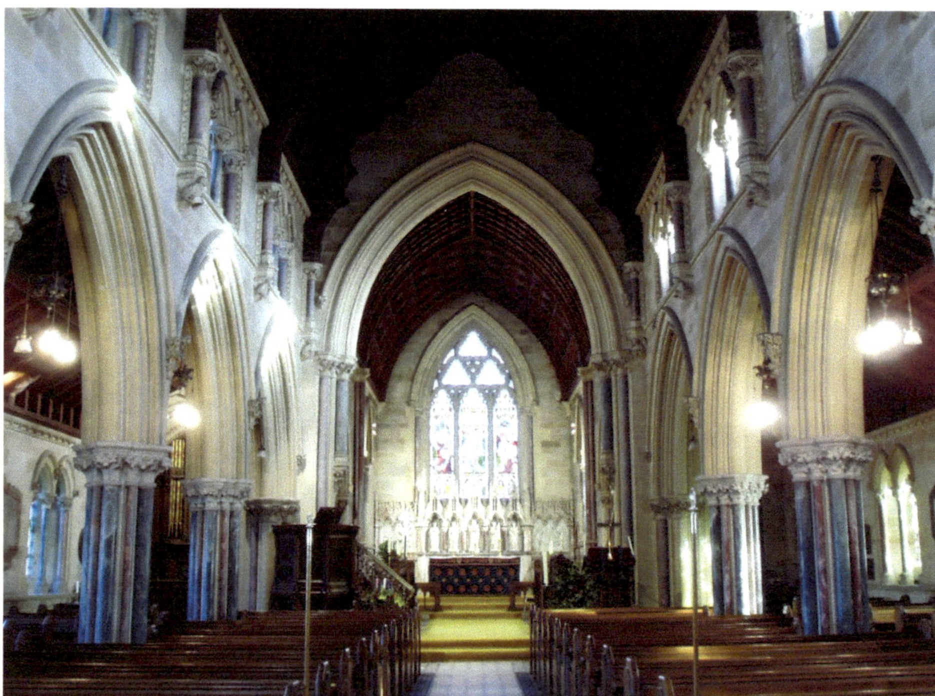

The opulent interior of George Gilbert Scott's fine All Saints' Church, Sherbourne, of 1862–64, a 'no expense spared' church replete with coloured marbles for the nave columns.

and a vaulted organ chamber to the north. There are many tablets to the Ryland family around the walls and a full complement of stained glass by Clayton & Bell, Heaton Butler & Bayne and Hardman.

51. Stoneleigh, St Mary

One of the most ancient and interesting churches in the county, St Mary's is still largely a twelfth-century Norman building with later additions, most apparent on the north side of the nave where a blocked Norman doorway with a worn tympanum carved with beasts can be found between windows enlarged in the fourteenth century. The sturdy tower too is Norman in its lower stages, with an oddly narrow top storey added in the fifteenth century. The nave has a single side aisle on the south side added in the fourteenth century, with a chapel to its east (now the vestry) built in 1665 with a bizarrely raised roof. Finally, a much larger chapel was added to the north side in 1823 to serve as a mausoleum for the Leigh family.

The interior still feels much as it did in the 1800s thanks to the box pews in the nave and gallery at the west end. The focal point is the richly decorated Norman chancel arch with chevron mouldings (surprisingly re-cut in places with small griffin and serpent motifs). The chancel beyond is dark and mysterious with pilasters either side suggesting a vault was originally intended. Here are gathered the best monuments in the church, although the Dudley monument to the left of the altar is rather overpowering. The single most important furnishing here is the Norman font in the south aisle, said to have come from Maxstoke Priory and carved with the figures of Apostles in niches.

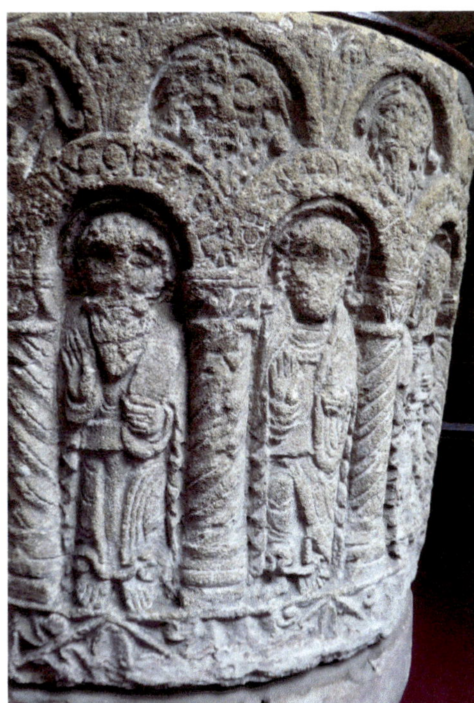

Detail of St Mary's twelfth-century Norman font, reputedly found in the ruins of Maxstoke Priory and subsequently brought to Stoneleigh. The figures appear to depict the Apostles.

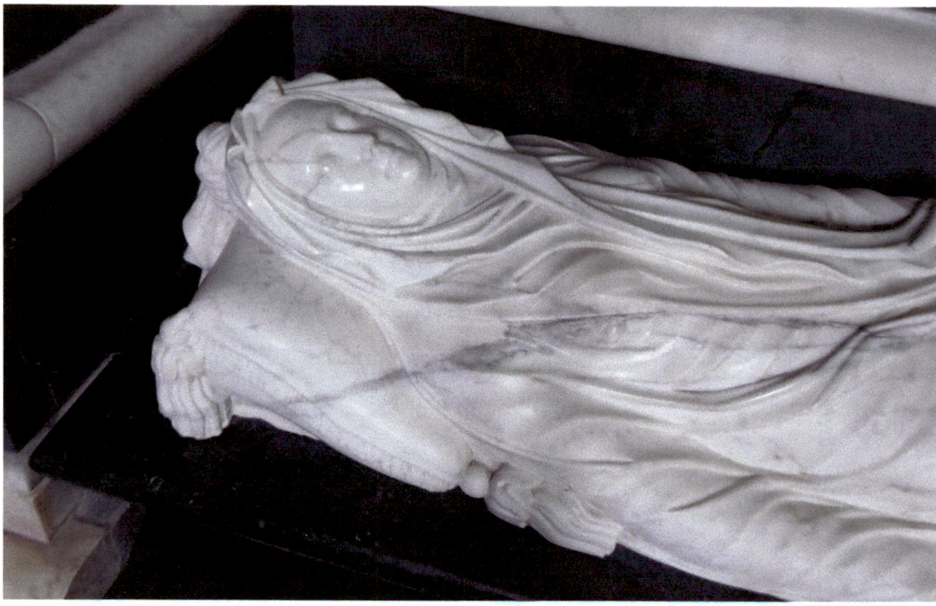

Detail of the black and white marble monument of 1648 with shrouded effigies of Alice, Duchess of Dudley and her daughter (shown here). The monument on a whole is anything but subtle, but the effigies themselves are rather fine.

Of the aforementioned monuments that to Alice Duchess of Dudley (d. 1688) and her daughter is the most notable, although it is a rather inelegant thing, a huge mass of black and white marble dominating the sanctuary. The marble effigies of the mother and daughter lying separately in their shrouds are, however, beautifully carved. The 1850 Chandos Leigh memorial opposite takes the form of an alabaster tomb-chest within a vaulted recess. Of the two medieval effigies the fourteenth-century priest lying in the chancel is the far better preserved; the fourteenth-century lady lying in the porch beneath the tower is so badly worn as to have lost all its detail.

52. Stratford-upon-Avon, Holy Trinity

One of the most visited churches in the country needs little introduction, famous the world over as the last resting place of a certain celebrated local playwright! It is, however, a more than worthy building regardless of the Shakespeare connection and one of the grandest parish churches in the country.

The central tower with its distinctive rose windows dates back to *c.* 1210, but most of this imposing cruciform building is the result of major fourteenth- and fifteenth-century rebuilding, resulting in the nave receiving its handsome clerestories and a new chancel enriched with huge Perpendicular windows. The west window of the nave was also enlarged and a vaulted north porch added which has served as the main entrance ever since. The present spire was built in 1763, replacing a wooden predecessor, aside from that the only post-Reformation addition to the church is the vestry extension added to the south side in 2016.

The interior is still mostly defined by the late medieval alterations, the nave rising splendidly to a fine panelled roof and the clerestories flooding the space with light (the side aisles are still mainly fourteenth-century work). Beyond the crossing the sumptuous chancel forms a fitting climax, a fine example of Perpendicular Gothic under a richly carved roof. The late fifteenth century choir stalls have a fine set of carved misericords with engaging scenes, amusing heads and fanciful beasts. The walls are mostly glazed (the glass entirely Victorian aside from the surviving medieval traceries of the south-east window), leaving less room for monuments, thus a couple (including Shakespeare's) have invaded the window openings while others surround the sanctuary.

The oldest tomb is to Dean Balsall (d. 1491), who built the chancel, sadly without its brass and its sculptures thoroughly mutilated. The collection of family monuments in the Clopton Chapel in the north aisle, colourful tombs with effigies of Tudor and Elizabethan date, is the most imposing in the church (the rest of the church's surviving medieval glass can also be seen here gathered into the north

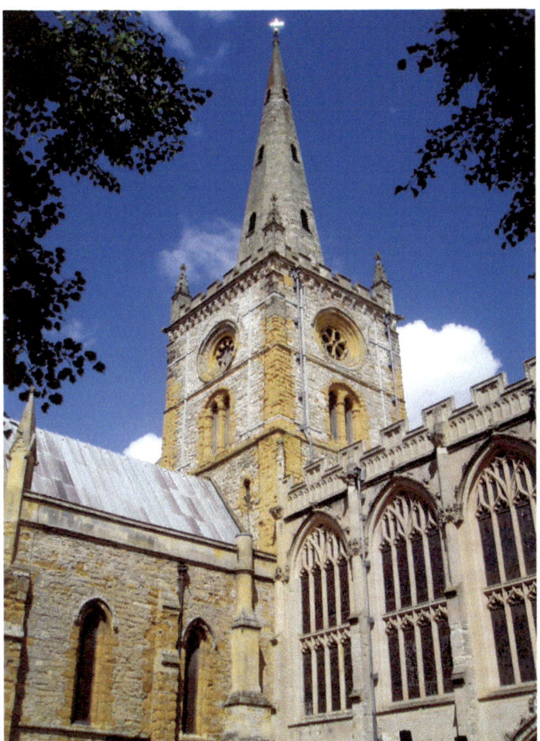

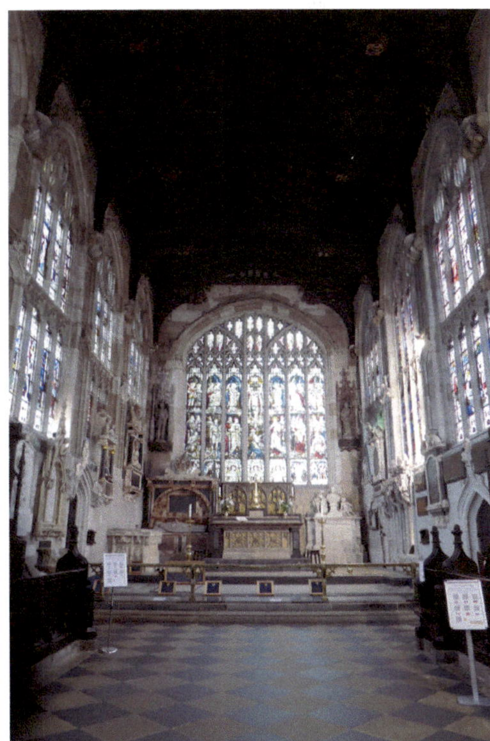

Above left: Holy Trinity Church, Stratford-upon-Avon. The central tower of *c*. 1210 with its distinctive rose-window apertures is the earliest part of the present church. The spire is a rebuilding of 1763 of its wooden predecessor.

Above right: Holy Trinity's late medieval chancel is the most impressive part of the interior and a good example of the Perpendicular style. William Shakespeare's memorial and grave are situated to the left of the main altar.

window). There are many notable later memorials in the chancel, including of course William Shakespeare's bust poetically overlooking his own grave in the sanctuary.

53. Stratford-upon-Avon, Guild Chapel of the Holy Cross

The Guild Chapel has been owned by the Corporation since 1553, but originally served the thirteenth-century Guild of the Holy Cross whose members included several men of high status. This late medieval two-cell church without aisles thus had considerable expense thrown at it, as witnessed by the impressive late fifteenth-century nave with its tall Perpendicular windows. The handsome north porch and west tower belong to the same phase, while the chancel is an earlier and much more humble structure.

The interior is the showpiece here, basking in the light from the tall nave windows and culminating in a fragmentary painting of the Last Judgement over the chancel arch – the flat eighteenth-century plaster ceiling cuts off the topmost part, but heads of Christ and angels have been found above it. Originally the whole interior was richly painted, many more fragments were uncovered in 1804 in the chancel and elsewhere, these sadly since lost or re-covered (most were recorded in detail).

The nave was formerly adorned on the north side with a cycle of the Dance of Death (a stark reminder of human mortality, whatever one's status) and on the south with the Life of Adam. Fragments remain today of these schemes, though

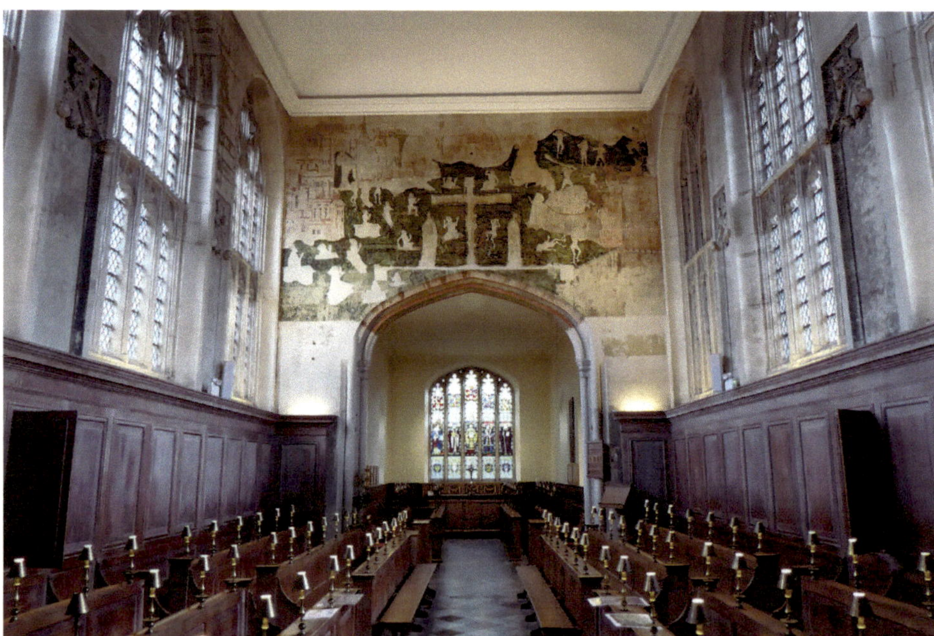

Guild Chapel of the Holy Cross, Stratford-upon-Avon. The late fifteenth-century nave with the remains of the Last Judgement or 'Doom' painting over the chancel arch, around ghostly shapes of a Crucifixion group marking where the original rood-screen figures would have been.

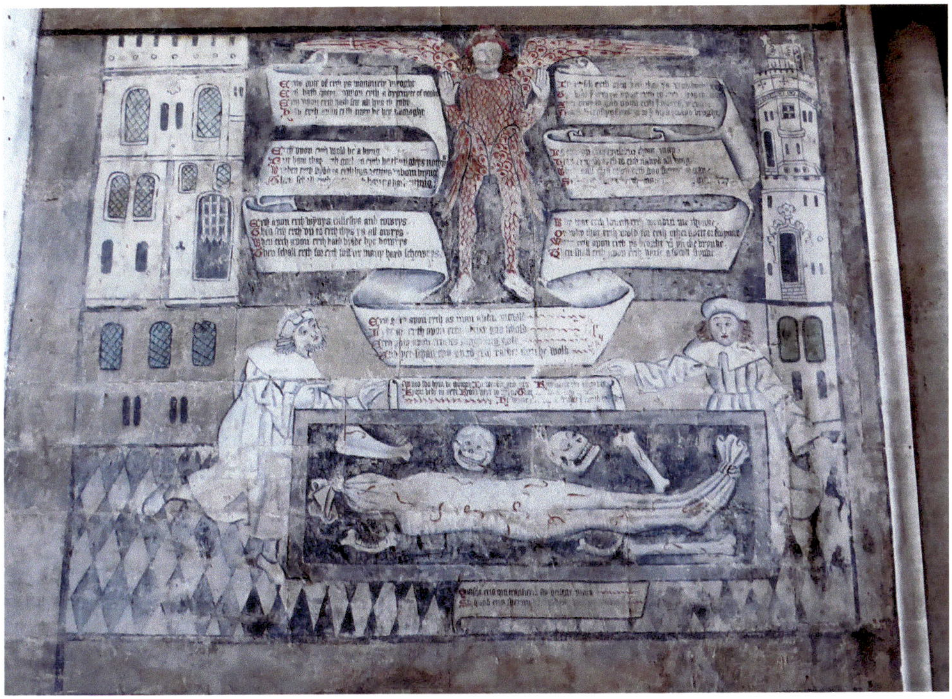

'Erthe upon Erthe', a popular medieval poem and allegory of death. This well-preserved mural with an angel above a grisly grave scene was uncovered in 2016.

most is hidden by the present collegiate-style seating and panelling; a couple of panels have been opened recently to give a glimpse of what remains behind them. The best-preserved painting was only uncovered as recently as 2016 behind panelling at the west end and depicts the popular medieval poem 'Erthe upon Erthe', an allegory of death, with an angel above and a grisly body in a grave below.

54. Tredington, St Gregory

Tredington Church is one of the most impressive in south Warwickshire, a beautifully hued fourteenth-century building distinguished by a graceful spire (crowning an already tall tower) at the west end that dominates this pretty village. The exterior is all of a piece aside from a chevron-decorated Norman doorway on the south side; entry, however, is normally via a much grander north porch.

Within, the earlier history of the church is more apparent, with substantial remains of blocked Saxon windows embedded in the masonry immediately above the nave arcades, showing how these were cut through the ancient walling in the late twelfth/early thirteenth century, retaining parts of the previous clerestory in the process, which then would once have been hidden beneath plaster and mural decoration.

There is much ancient woodwork in this church: most of the pews are medieval with decorative panelling, as is the chancel screen, while nearby is a handsome

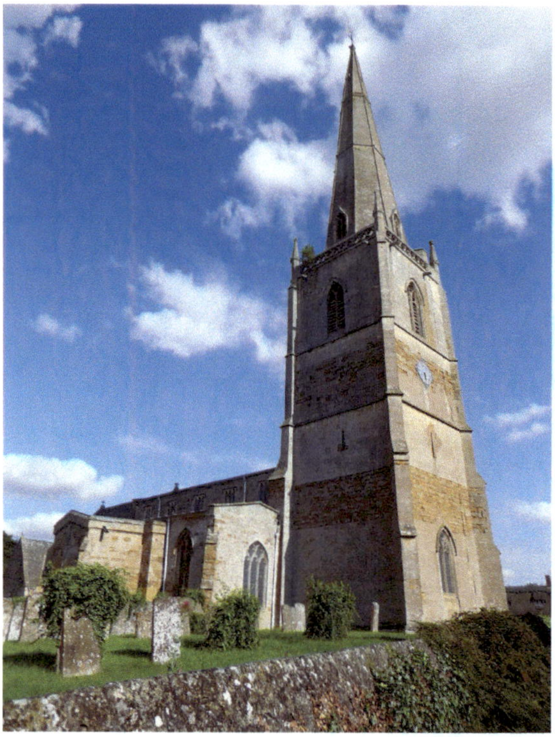

Left: The handsome fourteenth-century tower and spire of St Gregory's, Tredington, seen from the north-west.

Below: The nave of *c*. 1200 with Transitional arches and columns, cut through a much earlier Anglo-Saxon wall with traces of ancient windows still visible embedded above the arches. The nave pews and screen are mostly fifteenth century.

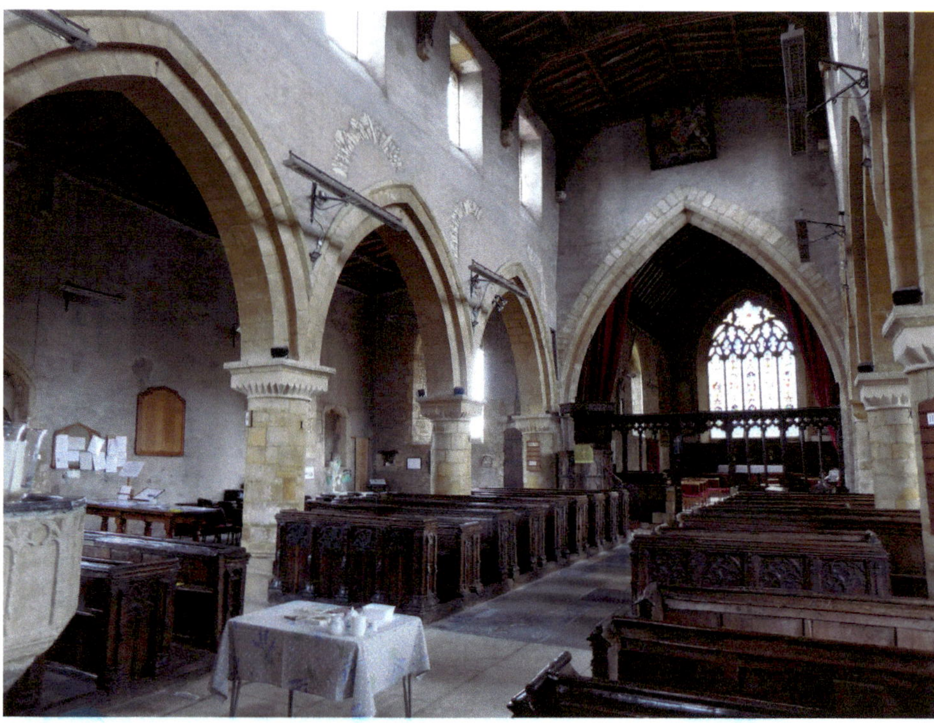

Jacobean pulpit. There are fine fifteenth-century brasses to a kneeling Henry Sampson and an unknown priest, now mounted at the west end. Best of all is the delightful sense of antiquity this church has retained in its largely unrestored interior, the only obvious Victorian impact being the glass in the chancel.

55. Tysoe, Assumption

Tysoe Church is sometimes referred to as St Mary's, but its proper dedication is to the Assumption of the Blessed Virgin Mary, one of those rare dedications once popular in pre-Reformation England. It is one of the grandest and most attractive churches in south Warwickshire with beautiful honey-hued stonework adding to its appeal.

The overall impression externally is of a later medieval building with large Perpendicular traceried windows in the chancel, an extraordinarily long nave clerestory (beneath an ornate parapet) and the topmost stage of the tower all suggesting a major fifteenth-century remodelling of the structure. Above the chancel arch is a rare Sanctus bell turret, though its present form is the result of seventeenth-century repair, while the aisles below suggest a fourteenth-century date with their handsome windows and carved friezes. The core of the church, however, is considerably older, much of it late Norman or Transitional while some elements date back to Saxon times. Entry is via the south porch through a fine late Norman doorway with unusual mouldings and an Agnus Dei carving above.

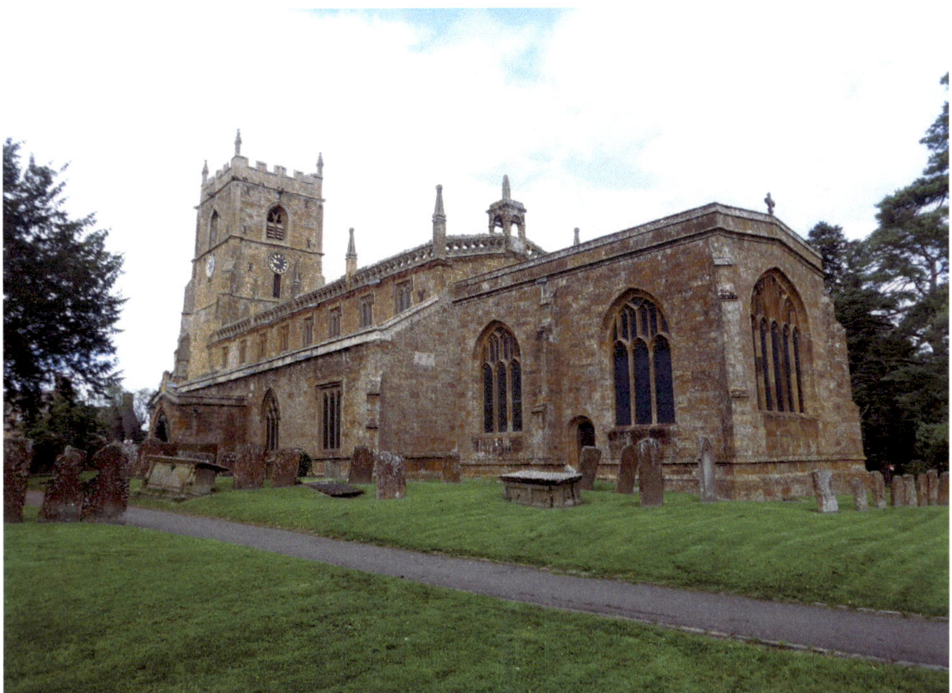

Tysoe's church as seen from the south-east, most of which appears to be the result of a major fifteenth-century remodelling of the structure, but the core of the building is much earlier.

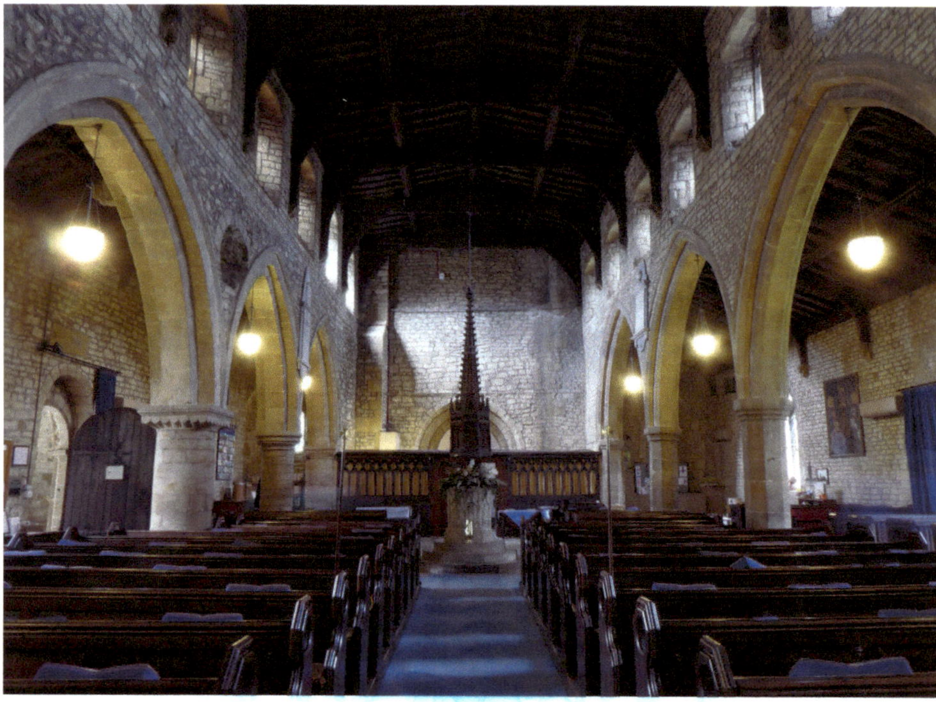

View of the nave looking westwards towards the towering font cover. The south arcade to the left is cut through an eleventh-century wall with the remains of two ancient windows still embedded above the arches.

The interior was stripped of plaster (or 'scraped') in the Victorian restoration exposing the stonework everywhere, which, while attractively coloured, renders the church a little dark within. One benefit of this was the discovery of the two Anglo-Saxon window recesses above the south arcade with elements of herringbone masonry. The arcades themselves while pointed are clearly of the Transitional period judging by the Norman style of the nave columns and capitals. There are interesting corbel carvings throughout the church, but the most striking interior feature is the medieval font whose tapering cover (a more recent restoration) dominates the west end of the nave. The fourteenth-century octagonal basin has crudely carved but still recognisable figures of saints under canopies adorning its sides.

56. Warmington, St Michael

Warmington Church stands proud on high ground with its tower overlooking the main road up the north-eastern fringe of Edgehill. It is of mainly early thirteenth- to fourteenth-century date and built of the local ironstone, which always adds such character with its delightful golden-brown hue.

The pleasing colouring of the stonework is also most apparent inside both nave and aisles, which are separated by solid Transitional-style arcades (effectively Norman pillars carrying pointed arches). There is some interesting tracery in the

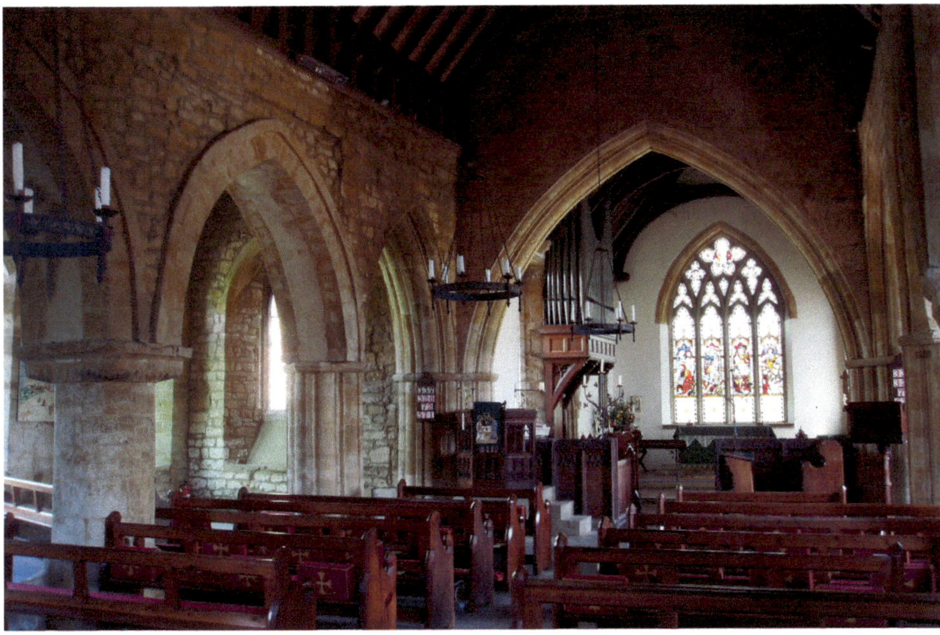

St Michael's Church, Warmington. View of the Transitional nave of *c.* 1200 (with Norman pillars carrying pointed arches) and the fourteenth-century chancel beyond.

north aisle, particularly the pentagram design in the east window. Beyond the lower part of the fifteenth-century rood screen, the chancel betrays detailing from the fourteenth century, most notably the exuberant sedilia with its richly cusped ogee canopies. The priest's door opposite leads to the remarkable two-storey vestry, easily missed inside but externally a much more noticeable structure. Its lower floor was a chapel while the upper chamber was the priest's room, replete with a barred opening into the church looking over the main altar.

There are few memorials of note (though some more handsome ones in the churchyard) and Clayton & Bell glass in the chancel (and Holt of Warwick's poor west window). The nave fortunately remains plain-glazed, for it is a dark and mysterious space redolent with history.

57. Warwick, St Mary

St Mary's Church, Warwick, is a vast and imposing edifice, easily one of the most rewarding in the entire country. It was half destroyed by the fire that swept through the town in 1694 losing its nave and transepts, but luckily the most important parts, the chancel and Beauchamp Chapel survived. The nave, transepts and tower were rebuilt by Sir William Wilson in an unusual but not unattractive synthesis of Gothic and classical style, the soaring west tower being a particular success and a landmark for miles around.

The imposing chancel was completed at the very end of the fourteenth century and is a good early example of the Perpendicular style. At its centre is the impressive alabaster tomb of Thomas Beauchamp, Earl of Warwick (builder of this chancel and grandfather of Richard, who built the adjoining Beauchamp Chapel) with his wife on a large tomb-chest surrounded by many small mourner figures. The most dramatic feature is the vaulted ceiling with its 'flying ribs', which support a flatter, but otherwise more conventional vault with a somewhat skeletal look.

To the north lie vaulted vestries and a chapter house (mostly obscured by the huge Greville monument that fills it) and from here the wonderfully rare Norman crypt can be entered. This remarkable space dates from 1123 and covers the space beneath the chancel, here split into two aisles by immensely thick pillars supporting hefty, vaulted ceilings.

The gorgeous Beauchamp Chapel to the south is one of the best-preserved medieval interiors in England. The chapel is rich in excellent monuments. The tomb of the chapel's founder, Richard Beauchamp, is the centrepiece, with magnificent gilt bronze sculptures and Richard's effigy lying resplendent in armour beneath a cage-like frame for his funeral pall, while the tomb-chest below is adorned with figures of family members and small angels.

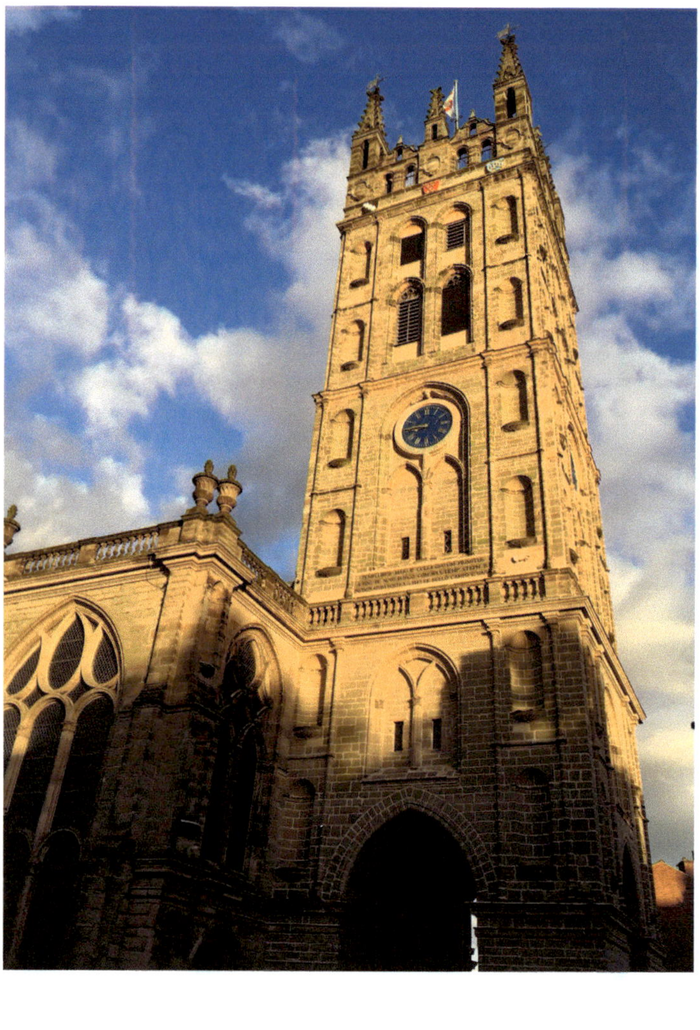

The handsome west tower of St Mary's Church, Warwick, completed *c.* 1704. It was originally intended to build the tower within the new nave but a weakness in the structure resulted in the present tower projecting dramatically into the street, its base acting as an entrance porch, open on three sides.

Equally spectacular is the delightful east window, which is filled with superb fifteenth-century glass by John Prudde, the king's glazier. Much of it is not in situ, since Cromwell's troops wrought havoc with the glass here and the surviving figures were assembled in this window (only the outer pairs of figures in the upper row are in their original positions). The north and south windows retain original glass only in their traceries and the cusped heads of the main lights, and knowing the quality of the surviving elements makes this loss all the more grievous.

A further treasure and miraculous survivor of Puritan fanatics is the statuary surrounding the east window. This unique display of almost perfectly preserved figure sculpture from the early fifteenth century is exquisite, mostly depicting angels and four female saints (an answer to all those empty niches we see in medieval churches elsewhere). The medieval splendour is further echoed by the use of colour on the sculptures and vaulted ceiling, all tastefully redone in the mid-twentieth century but based on medieval precedents.

The later monuments should not be overlooked, nor indeed would that be even possible since the tomb of Robert Dudley, Earl of Leicester (d. 1588) and

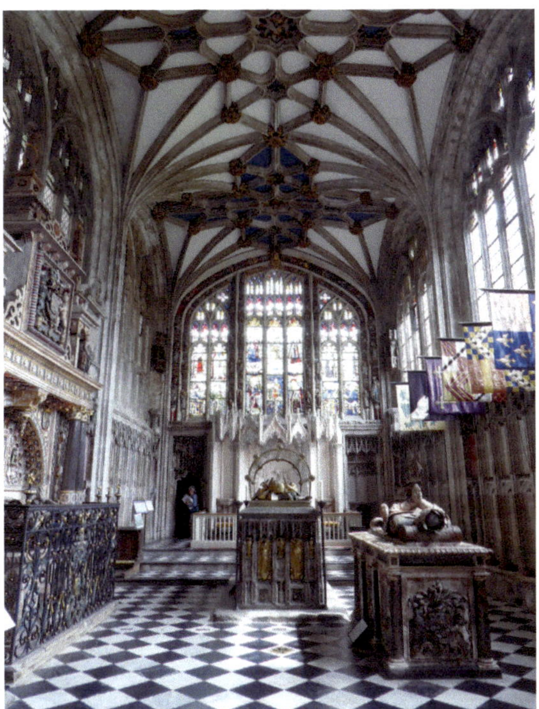

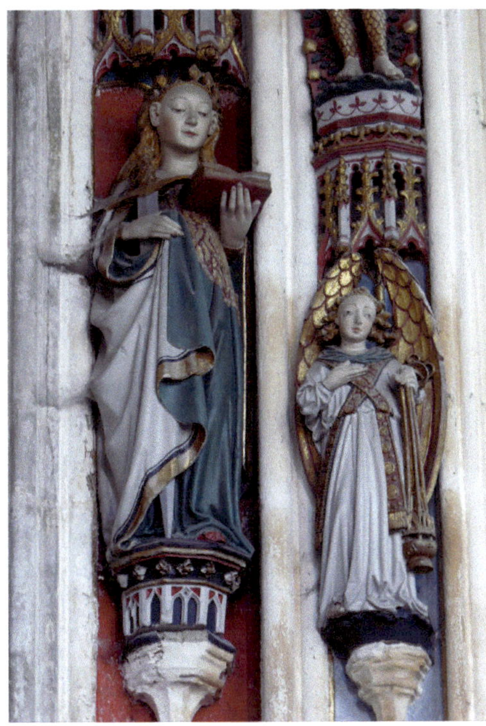

Above left: The stunning Beauchamp Chapel is the chantry of Sir Richard Beauchamp (whose tomb occupies the centre) and the showpiece of St Mary's. It is also one of the best-preserved late medieval interiors in England, replete with superb stained glass, statuary and outstanding monuments.

Above right: St Catherine and an angel, two of the multitude of carved figures surrounding the east window of the Beauchamp Chapel, an extremely rare survival. Four female saints are included along with the Nine Orders of Angels.

favourite of Elizabeth I, dominates the north side with its towering canopy, rich in Renaissance splendour. The tomb and effigy of his elder brother Ambrose, Earl of Warwick stands nearby while the poignant diminutive tomb of Robert Dudley's young son ('the noble impe') lies beside the altar.

Lastly, the visitor should not miss the tiny Dean's Chapel, sandwiched between the Beauchamp Chapel and the chancel (entered from the latter), a delightful late medieval room covered by a confectionary-like miniature fan vault.

58. Weston-on-Avon, All Saints

This small, neat church won't delay the visitor for long but has a great deal of charm; its beautifully hued exterior would look at home in the Cotswolds and indeed the village was only transferred from Gloucestershire in 1931.

The interior is flooded with light from the remarkable Perpendicular north nave windows, an almost continuous wall of glass and mullions with painted and stained medieval quarries surviving in one of them (each depicting a canopied boat, a donor's rebus). The two large south windows are actually a blocked arcade that once led into a demolished side chapel to which a large diagonal squint in the chancel once connected.

The attractive wooden furnishings are mostly early twentieth century, but earlier features include medieval floor tiles and two small but very finely detailed mid-sixteenth-century Grevill brasses in the sanctuary.

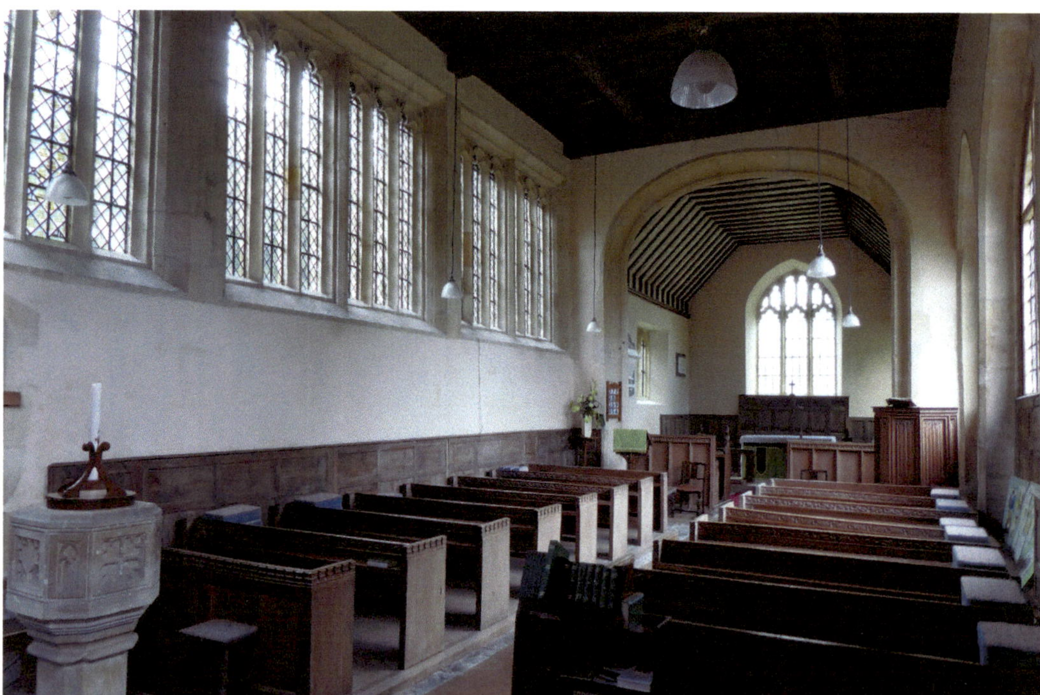

The charmingly simple interior of Weston church, with its unique row of large six-light Perpendicular windows illuminating the north side.

59. WHICHFORD, ST MICHAEL

An oasis of peace nestling in the hills of south Warwickshire, Whichford, possesses one of its more ancient and rewarding churches, dating back to Norman times as witnessed by its Romanesque south doorway with plain tympanum. However, most of the present building dates from the thirteenth to fifteenth centuries, the earlier phase represented by the plain west tower and the later by the fine nave clerestory. The nave has aisles of differing lengths, that on the south side being a mere chapel adjoining the porch.

Within the asymmetry of the aisles is more apparent, with a four-bay thirteenth-century arcade on the north side balanced by a single-arched opening to the south, leading into the Mohun Chapel. The whole interior is light and airy thanks to the plastered finish and the south clerestory flooding the nave with light, and it has an atmosphere of antiquity and charm.

Medieval stained glass is located around the church in small quantities, the earliest being in the north aisle, including three early fourteenth-century heraldic roundels. The chancel windows all retain their original fourteenth-century glass in their tracery lights, while best pieces can be found in the Mohun Chapel where the east window retains its full set of mid-fourteenth century traceries, including a fine head of Christ and an incomplete coronation of Mary. Here also a grave slab carved with a quartered shield of the Mohun family dating from *c.* 1300.

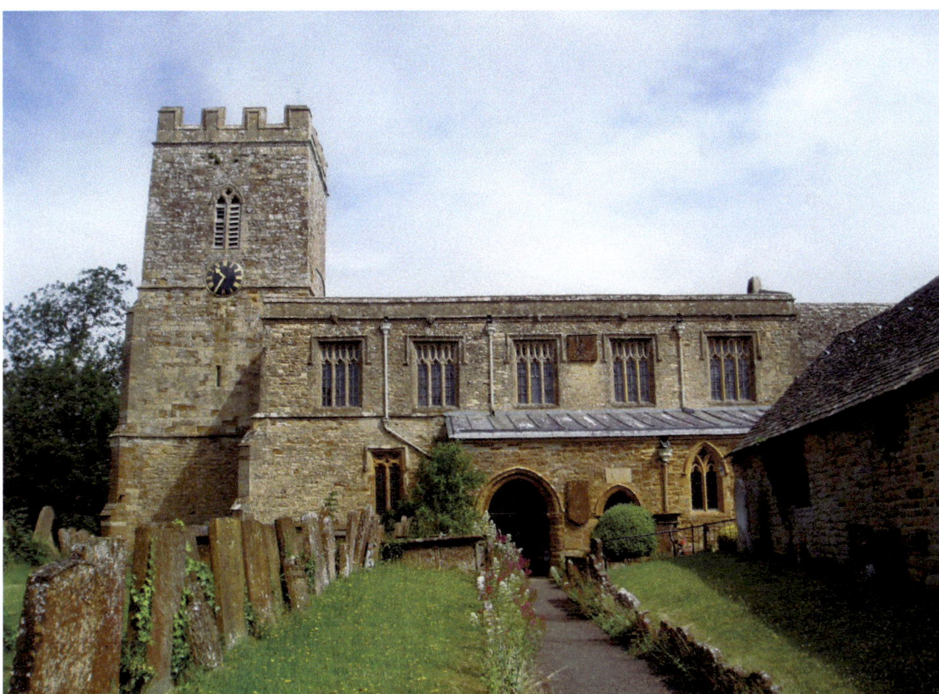

The picturesque St Michael's Church, Whichford, viewed from the south, showing the attractive clerestory added to the nave in the fifteenth century. The south porch does not project and instead is embedded into the short south aisle.

On the north side of the chancel is the most impressive tomb in the church, a late fifteenth-century tomb-chest under an arched recess with an incised slab of a priest lying under a rich canopy with chalice and book either side of his head. To the south lies another tomb-chest with an unusual synthesis of Gothic and Renaissance styles with an undersized brass to Rector Nicholas Asheton (*c.* 1582).

60. Wootton Wawen, St Peter

An impressive building, one of Warwickshire's oldest and most remarkable churches, the central tower being a fairly complete Anglo-Saxon structure in its lower stages crowned by a fifteenth-century belfry. The present church has grown around this, the nave a Norman structure expanded to include a south aisle in the thirteenth century and raised in the fifteenth to allow a handsome four-window clerestory on either side. The chancel and ample south chapel are mostly of fourteenth-century date with later alterations such as the large Perpendicular east window. The north side of the church by contrast appears somewhat stark and naked without the embrace of aisle or chapel.

Stepping inside the view eastwards down the nave comes as a bit of a shock as one sees a largely blank wall, the tower effectively cutting the church in half and blocking all view of the chancel beyond save for a small glimpse through the tiny eleventh-century arches that pierce its base. The effect is relieved by the

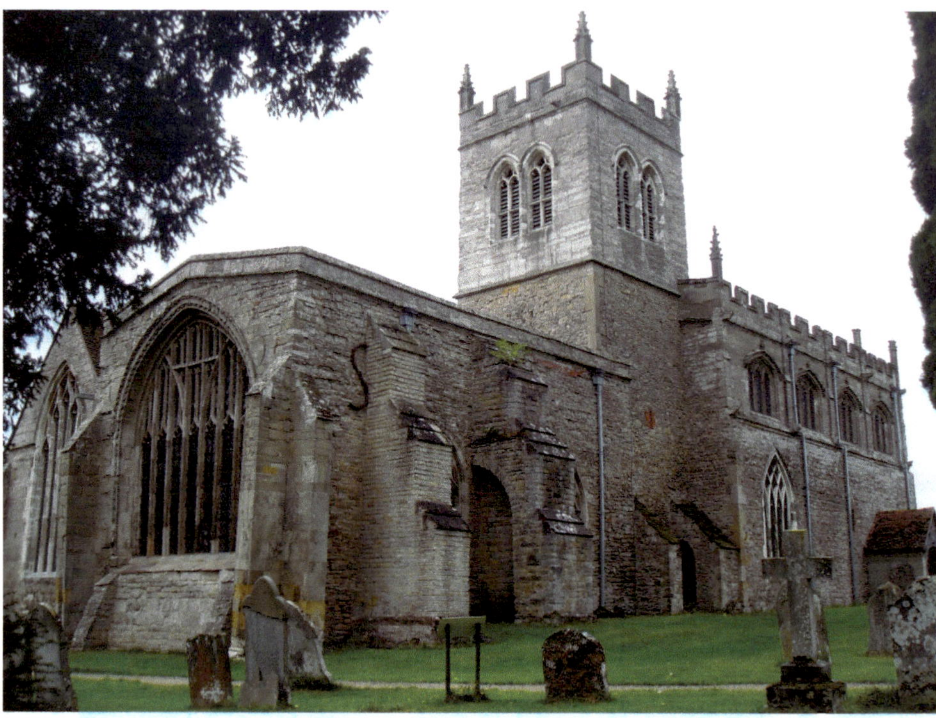

St Peter's Church, Wootton Wawen, viewed from the north-east and showing the exposed lower section of the tower dating back to the pre-Conquest period (perhaps tenth or eleventh century).

rare survival of two late medieval parclose screens jutting out into the nave with a connecting screen behind. The space under the tower beyond is as the Saxon builders left it, with a small arched opening on each side (that to the north now blocked and partially glazed). The chancel is well lit by the large east window which contains fragments of fifteenth-century glass including some good angel heads (earlier glass can be seen in the nave). The more rustically finished south chapel has traces of wall-painting, though what remains is largely covered by a profusion of wall tablets.

The chancel contains two medieval tombs, one with an alabaster effigy of a fifteenth-century knight, the other a tomb-chest with brasses to John Harewell (d. 1505) and his wife. In the south chapel lies the stiff and awkward armoured effigy of Francis Smith (d. 1606) surrounded by an ornate Jacobean canopy with various wall memorials nearby, including a huge eighteenth century one to the Knight family that rather dominates the space.

Other features of note include the fourteenth-century octagonal font with rustic carved head corbels at the angles (similar fonts appear at Lapworth and Snitterfield) and nearby two striking corbel heads of a king and queen flanking the Perpendicular west window. Lastly a small piece of modern stained glass by Margaret Traherne cheers the lunette of the blocked north doorway under the tower, enlivening this otherwise stark space.

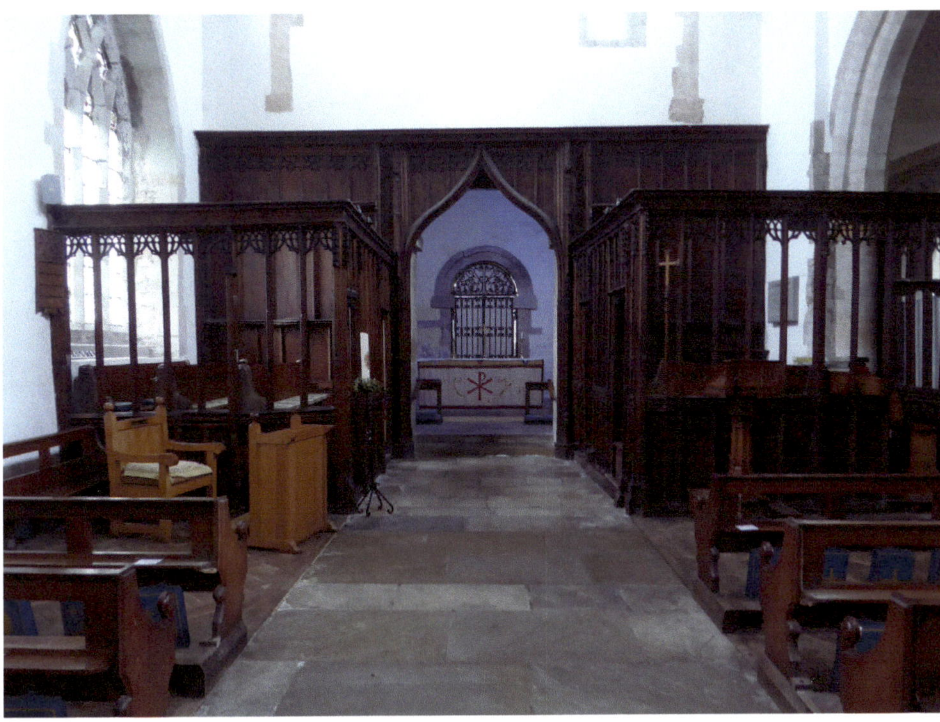

View of the fifteenth-century parclose screens at the east end of the nave which would have formed separate pews or chapels. The simple Anglo-Saxon east doorway of the tower is visible through the central arch of the screen.

ACKNOWLEDGEMENTS

I am deeply indebted to the following individuals for their assistance in the preparation of this book, most particularly a huge thanks to my sister Elspeth Thomson for several excursions driving all around Warwickshire to revisit various churches included in this book. A big thanks to Mark and Fiona Russell for trips out to Chesteron and Lower Shuckburgh.

I am very grateful to the following for opening churches for me: Revd Carole Young at Merevale, Revd Paul Wikinson at Newbold, Father Stephen Day at Lillington and Jenny Scragg at Cheylesmore. Also, a big thanks to Helen Bryant at St Andrew's, Rugby and Susan and Clara at Holy Trinity in Stratford-upon-Avon for being so helpful and hospitable during my visit.